Tails of the Heart

Sherry Bennett Warshauer

PublishAmerica
Baltimore

First printing

Cover photo courtesy of American Kennel Club/photographer Mary Bloom.

Author photo courtesy of David Saperstein.

ISBN: 1-4241-5300-X
PUBLISHED BY PUBLISHAMERICA, LLLP
www.publishamerica.com
Baltimore

Printed in the United States of America

For Adam Zachary and James Andrew
And Matthew J., my husband, my rock.

PREFACE

Describing her first walk as a team with her Guiding Eyes dog Gardenia, Cecilia beamed with joy. "It was like walking fast and on air—like flying! I'm free!"

Guiding Eyes for the Blind is dedicated to enriching the lives of blind and visually impaired men and women by providing them with the freedom to travel safely, thereby assuring greater independence, dignity and new horizons of opportunity.

An independent, non-profit organization, it is considered to be one of the leading guide dog schools in the world. An amazing 6,000 Guiding Eyes teams have graduated from Guiding Eyes for the Blind since its establishment in 1954. When teamed up with a professionally trained dog, Guiding Eyes graduates enjoy a higher level of participation in the activities of daily living. A guide dog has a remarkable positive impact on the life of its blind or visually impaired partner.

The cost of preparing each student/Guiding Eyes dog team is approximately $40,000 and is provided at no cost to the students. Guiding Eyes includes the provision of dogs, extensive training, travel costs, room and board for twenty-six days and lifetime follow-up services for its blind/visually impaired clients. The organization relies on the support of others, including volunteers. There are now more than 1,200 volunteers supporting Guiding Eyes for the Blind nationwide. Supporters and volunteers give tirelessly of their time and resources and are truly the unsung heroes of the organization. For that generosity and kindness, Guiding Eyes is forever grateful.

TABLE OF CONTENTS

INTRODUCTION

My first book, *Everyday Heroes*—published in the summer of 1998 by Howell Book House, then a division of MacMillan—received the 1999 Maxwell Award, an honor given for excellence in its category; and was the Book of the Month Club favorite for more than a year. Its success proved that there is significant public interest in non-fiction dog stories.

Tails of the Heart (stories for the dog lover in all of us) includes true stories about the dogs of Guiding Eyes for the Blind; guide dogs; Bureau of Alcohol, Tobacco, Firearms and Explosives (ATF); State Police Patrol and Detection dogs who work daily for our safety and protection; therapy dogs who help families in pain; release dogs who bring love to their families; and stories about raisers and their pups, honoring the loving relationship between people and these exceptional dogs. Several of the stories relate to 9/11. *Tails of the Heart* celebrates these dog teams.

My mission is to raise public awareness of the many ways service dogs enhance people's lives, and of the work of Guiding Eyes for the Blind, the organization that breeds, raises and trains the amazing animals in these stories.

As with *Everyday Heroes*, I am grateful to have had this opportunity to donate all of my time and income from this endeavor to Guiding Eyes for the Blind, to help them with their significant work. With special thanks to Jane Russenberger for her wisdom and guidance, and her always helpful staff at the Canine Development Center.

SERVICE DOGS

PART FIVE

Bibliographical Note

General bibliographies dealing with American farmers and farming are Everett E. Edwards, *A Bibliography of the History of Agriculture in the United States* (Washington, D.C. 1930. Reprinted, Detroit, Mich. 1967) and John T. Schlebecker, *A Bibliography of Books and Pamphlets on the History of Agriculture in the United States . . . 1607–1967* (Santa Barbara, Calif. 1969). Dennis S. Nordin, *A Preliminary List of References for the History of the Granger Movement* (Davis, Calif., 1967) is reasonably complete on the subject to the date of publication. George H. Miller, *Railroads and the Granger Laws* (Madison, Wis. 1971) provides additional material in the bibliographic essay, pp. 263–286. Denton E. Morrison, ed., *Farmers' Organizations and Movements: Research Needs and a Bibliography of the United States and Canada* (Research Bulletin, Agricultural Experiment Station, East Langing, Mich.) offers an extensive list of books, articles and pamphlets on farmer organizations in the United States. Carl C. Taylor, *The Farmers' Movement, 1620–1920* (New York, N.Y. 1953) includes a wide ranging bibliography. Robert L. Tontz, "Membership of General Farmers' Organizations, United States, 1874–1860," *Agricultural History* 38:143–156 (July 1964) brings together useful figures showing the size of farmer organizations.

Liberty Hyde Bailey, ed., *Cyclopedia of American Agriculture: A Popular Survey of Agricultural Conditions, Practices and Ideals in the United States and Canada,* 4 volumes,

BUREAU OF ALCOHOL, TOBACCO, FIREARMS AND EXPLOSIVES

Cascade/Special Agent Chilcott

Cascade, a four-year-old yellow Labrador sporting her ATF ID, walked down the ramp onto the commercial airliner. She and Special Agent Canine Handler Craig Chilcott were on their way to Colombine, Colorado. It was April of 1999, and they were responding to the tragic disaster at Colombine High School. Just an hour before, they had been sitting in a plush Washington, D.C. hotel being briefed to do explosives detection security sweeps of the room set aside for dignitaries who would be attending NATO's fiftieth anniversary celebration.

Their presence at Colombine High School was urgent. Their role was to locate explosives that had or had not been detonated, and to secure the crime scene enabling the Colorado Bureau of Investigation (CSI) to access the site.

The search revealed a target-rich environment. Large quantities of explosives, cartridges, and shells were all over the school. For two weeks they searched every locker, bag, closet and desk.

The crime scene took its toll on everyone's emotions. The sadness was palpable. Craig gave Cascade a chance to rest by visiting the Red Cross tent. People stopped to play and talk with Cascade. Having Cascade there helped to create a sense of normalcy. It made them think about their own dogs and relieved the intensity of the moment. Her antics made people laugh.

In October of 1997, Craig entered ATF K-9 explosives training school. He was paired with Cascade, then eighteen months old. Craig loved her from the start. Cascade had been released from Guiding Eyes for the Blind's guide dog program for being too distracted. Cascade had been trained by an Egyptian team at Front Royal, Virginia, as part of their ATF canine trainers course.

The US State Department is working with Egypt and other foreign countries to assist them in the creation of dog and handler teams to expedite the development of their own anti-terrorist programs.

Back in the states, Cascade was called upon to find spent cartridges or bullets that would match a gun used in a double homicide-arson. The area to be searched was a fifty-acre, overgrown ranch the suspect had used for target practice, in order to zero in his weapon prior to committing the homicide. The arson investigators had found spent cartridges and bullets at the scene of the double homicide-arson. They hoped to find the same spent cartridges and bullets (projectiles—rounds that had been discharged from the firearm) at this fifty-acre site, linking it to the suspect. Their mission, during one very hot summer, was to search the ranch too see if they could find this evidence. It was like looking for a needle in a haystack. They searched for ten to fifteen minutes at a time because of the extreme heat, then gave Cascade a water break, and cooled her off in the air-conditioned vehicle. They used flags to mark the areas that had been searched. Cascade gave it her all. She was working for Craig—for their team. They located an area where target practice had occurred. She gave her passive alert, which means she sits as close as she can get to the odor. Her entire face changes, her tail wags, her eyes become more focused and she salivates. Investigators started digging, sifting through the dirt, and uncovered some projectiles and spent cartridges. Success: the lab reported they had a match.

The existence of these K-9's is a definite deterrent in the fight against terrorism. Would-be bombers/terrorists, who are familiar with their reputation, have been deterred or have been forced to become more innovative in their attempt to defeat them. The fact that some of these dogs have been put on "hit" lists, proves how feared they are by bombers/terrorists and the reason they are always well protected by the ATF.

Garrett/Special Agent Neely

As police in Egypt approached a suspected terrorist safe house, their American-trained dog sat down blocking their path to the front entrance, signaling that he had locked onto the scent of explosives. They cautiously walked around the building and entered through a back door. They found the front door booby-trapped with forty pounds of TNT.

A cable from the Egyptians to ATF (now the United States Department of Justice's Bureau of Alcohol, Tobacco, Firearms and Explosives) was clear, "Your dog saved the lives of eleven of our policemen today."

Under a nine-year-old counter-terrorism program funded by the US State Department, the ATF is training Labrador retrievers to recognize and detect the chemical components used in weapons and explosives. The dogs are then donated to various worldwide law enforcement agencies. This program involves seventeen countries including: Jordan, Egypt, Israel, Argentina, Australia, and Malaysia.

Special Agent Ray Neely has been with the ATF since 1992. In 1997 he joined the Explosive Detection Canine Unit with his partner Garrett, a five-and-a-half-year-old male, yellow Labrador retriever. One of their missions for the ATF was in Bogota, Colombia. Neely had been there nine years before for the State Department. Having lived in Bogota for two years, Neely felt very comfortable returning when the need arose. However, this trip was quite different. He now had a K-9 partner, Garrett.

While Neely was obtaining security clearance at the US embassy, Garrett began to pull on the leash in the direction of a black Labrador retriever who was being handled by a foreign service officer. When asked where his dog came from the officer replied, "Guiding Eyes for the Blind." Imagine his first day in a foreign country, and Garrett meets another dog from Guiding Eyes!

There are two factions threatening the stability of the Colombian government and safety of their people. For thirty years, guerilla groups and narcotics traffickers have controlled large parts of the country. Both groups use explosives to achieve their goals. One of the primary functions of the ATF's office in Colombia is to assist their government in dealing with this hazard.

Special Agent Neely and Garrett were in Bogota to assist the United States government with US embassy security. Neely was asked to do an unofficial assessment of Colombia's K-9 program. He determined that if they had well-trained American dogs they could become a more effective force.

Garrett has been trained not only to seek out bombs, but to recover evidence such as residue, bomb-making materials that have residue on them, and firearms that have been discarded or hidden. Only four months after graduating from his training class, Garrett was put to the test. He was asked to take part in a search following a bank robbery. The gunman had been apprehended. However, they needed to find the weapon which had been discarded. It took Garrett forty minutes to locate the gun under a bush. Garrett is a passive-alert dog, which means he sits upon finding the item, and looks to Neely. In order to make an arrest, it is necessary to link all items that have explosive residue back to the individual.

These dogs have proven themselves to be invaluable in keeping law and order and in our war against terrorists.

CONNECTICUT STATE POLICE

Dakota/Officer Proulx

It was past midnight. Officer William Proulx had completed an assignment and was headed home with his K-9 patrol dog Bruno sitting in the rear seat of their Connecticut State Police cruiser. Dakota, a six-month-old German shepherd in pre-training, was asleep beside Bruno.

The radio call broke their silence. A family had called for help. A burglar had invaded their home, a farmhouse in a rural part of the state, some fifteen miles away. Fearful that the burglar would hold the family hostage, the police needed to avoid a confrontation until the burglar was out of the house. Proulx was ordered to approach the scene in silence and to park away from the house. The K-9 team rolled up, with their lights out, and came to a stop about 300 feet from the house. At almost the same moment, a man began running through the woods, hopped the stone wall, and onto the road directly in front of the police cruiser. Instinctively, Proulx released Bruno. The shepherd closed the distance between him and the suspect and downed him in one flying leap. When Proulx reached them, Bruno had a lock hold on his prisoner's arm. To the officer's surprise, there was Dakota sitting on top of the burglar, looking very triumphant. Somehow that little scamp had exited the car and followed his mentor Bruno. A medical examination of the suspect is routine after an arrest of this nature. When the physician at the hospital examined the suspect, he asked about the series of small puncture wounds on his back. Proulx, realizing the marks came from Dakota's baby teeth, replied, "He must have fallen into rose bushes when he was brought down."

Bruno, a male German shepherd, was Proulx's first K-9 partner. He was a legend in his time, performing heroic deeds, and saving Proulx in life and death confrontations on more than one occasion. They took first place in the Connecticut State Police K-9 Olympics four years in a row, earning the status of best K-9 team in the state. Anticipating Bruno's future retirement, Proulx adopted six-month-old Dakota, with the intention of making a smooth transition. Proulx got Dakota ready for the next patrol dog training class, while Bruno was still working, but age was creeping up on him. In this stressful line of work, eight was the average age for K-9 retirement, depending upon the dog's physical condition.

When Proulx graduated with Dakota in November of 2000, he retired Bruno from the force, to become his pet. Shortly thereafter, Bruno showed signs of wear and tear. He developed spinal arthritis, hip dysplasia and deteriorated quickly. He died just before his tenth birthday.

Dakota's dark coloring gives him a fierce and wolf-like appearance. He is athletic and fast, and all muscle. He has an intense focus when tracking. When off duty, he is a playful pup. The sight of children makes him light up. He is all kisses.

Dakota and Bruno were the best of friends. They would play for hours on end. Dakota would sneak up behind, bite Bruno's tail and run. When Bruno caught him, Dakota would rollover on his back, and they would wrestle around the floor until they were exhausted.

Proulx remembers when Dakota was in training and accompanied him and Bruno on a case. It was a Saturday night when his department received a complaint that there were youngsters on the roof of a school. When Proulx arrived he found several girls sitting in parked cars. Their boyfriends had taken off. Extensive damage had been done to the air-conditioning unit and ducts on the roof. It was purposeless vandalism.

Having approached from the north, Proulx deduced that the boys must have headed south. He was eager to use Dakota, who had recently completed his training, but was a rookie in terms of experience. Proulx harnessed him up while an indignant Bruno began to destroy the car. Proulx decided it would be prudent to secure Bruno outside of the car. As Dakota walked alongside the school, his natural instincts kicked in. His head turned upward and then forward. Proulx knew he had gotten the track. They proceeded through the woods with Proulx carrying him over the stream (Dakota was unsure of the water). Then they raced through cornfields and out onto the sidewalk. Proulx spotted the boys fifty yards in front of them. He tried to close the 100-foot distance quietly, but one of the boys turned, saw him and broke into a run. Proulx yelled to them, "I've got Bruno, hit the ground, or I'll let him go." Being familiar with the dog and his reputation, they hit the ground. Dakota having tracked successfully, looked eagerly to Proulx for his reward: a tug-of-war with a "kong on a rope." While lying on the ground, one of the boys turned to look back at Proulx. There was Dakota lying on his back, wiggling around playing with his toy. Not exactly a vision that would evoke terror. Proulx, stalling for time, yelled out, "If you turn around, I'll let Bruno go. You know how crazy he is." Back-up arrived and the boys were taken into custody.

Officer Proulx received a call that a local storeowner had had his store vandalized. Proulx jumped into his patrol car with three-year-old Dakota, and went to investigate. Three young men had bullied the storeowner, smashed his windows, and took off. The owner of the store told Proulx he saw the men run across the street and through the grass. Proulx brought Dakota to the grassy spot, with the hope that no one else had walked there, thus contaminating the site. Dakota sniffed the grass, lifted his head to sniff the air, locked onto the scent and began to track. Proulx gave the command, "Find him." Dakota took Proulx over railroad tracks, through a parking lot and finally stopped in front of a pizza parlor. He began pacing back and forth, or "worrying" in front of the store. At first, Proulx didn't take this seriously, for he thought Dakota was more interested in the scent of pizza than in tracking. Proulx watched his K-9 carefully. Dakota persisted. Proulx looked through the windows of the pizza parlor and saw two of the three men whom the storeowner described as the perpetrators. The other people in the restaurant looked up at Proulx, with obvious interest in what was going on. The two patrons continued to eat their pizza, and sat with their eyes focused on the table. "That was a dead giveaway," according to Proulx. "The innocent always stare at the cops. If someone doesn't look at them, something is wrong." Proulx asked them to step outside where he questioned them, and ultimately made the arrest.

Proulx was called as back-up for an officer in pursuit of a car that was being driven suspiciously. Luckily the "bad guys" were stuck in traffic. The officer got out of his car and approached the car. The suspect exited his car, approached the officer, and lunged toward him. A struggle ensued. The suspect was making repeated attempts to get to the rear of his car, when Proulx arrived on the scene. He opened the driver's side window, gave Dakota the command, leaned to the right, while all eighty-five pounds of dog glided through the window over Proulx's left shoulder. Dakota ran past the police officer, got the suspect's arm in a vice-like grip, immobilizing him. Proulx calmly handcuffed him. Dakota instinctively never confuses the officers with the suspects. Proulx attributes that ability to discern the difference, to the smell of the equipment, uniform, or the police station they may have left hours ago. Or perhaps it is the familiarity of the officers who are always around him, playing with him.

When they opened the trunk of the car, they found an assault rifle with twenty- and thirty-round magazines. This arrest obviously frustrated a mission. There was no question that Dakota prevented a major disaster from occurring.

There was a 911 call. A woman was asking for a "ride home." The dispatcher sensed panic in the woman's voice. She may have been talking in code to prevent someone nearby from knowing she was calling for help. They dispatched a car terming the situation an "unknown problem," probably domestic. Proulx was in the middle of a robbery investigation nearby, and was called as back-up. The apartment the woman called from was two and a half stories up. The male party, who was wanted for parole violation, was cheating on his

21

girlfriend. The girlfriend had come home, found them together and a fight followed. The suspect was afraid of the police, so when the officer knocked at the door of the apartment, he jumped off the balcony and hit the ground running.

Proulx arrived a few minutes later with Dakota and began to track. Dakota scented the grassy area below. His nose shot up in the air, followed by whimpering and whining. This told Proulx that Dakota had the air scent. The scent flows off the person and is airborne. Dakota raced through the parking lot, around the cars, into the woods, back to the parking lot and under a parked truck. Moments later, Proulx heard the suspect scream. Dakota had taken hold of his arm and was dragging him out from under the truck.

Three-year-old Dakota and Proulx came in second in their first K-9 Olympics. They were one of the three teams of K-9 handlers and their dogs, from the Connecticut State Police, flown to Las Vegas to compete in a national competition. As a department, they came in second. Not bad, considering as many as sixty departments were represented. Proulx is very proud of his K-9 partner and of the East Hartford K-9 division.

Odin/Trooper Csontos

It was impossible to hide one's emotions under the circumstances. Dogs reflect their handlers' reaction. "All of your emotions flow down that leash. If the handler is stressed, the dog can read it. It took every ounce of inner strength to raise the spirits of my dog. His eyes searched mine for reassurance."

Their mission following the September 11 attack at the World Trade Center was to find survivors. They got their orders and went in. When he arrived at the site, Trooper First Class William Csontos, with the Connecticut State Police, was moved by the silence. There were so many people and so much activity, but the silence of death surrounded them. There was debris everywhere, covered by two inches of dust. He will never forget the smells of pulverized concrete and the eerie devastation of the buildings. It was like a war zone.

NYPD needed search and rescue teams immediately. Ten Connecticut State Police teams and six teams from New York State responded. Trooper Csontos and his K-9 partner Odin, a three-year-old German shepherd, arrived at the scene each day around 5:30 A.M. The workdays were never less than twelve hours and many times as long as seventeen hours. Five teams worked the morning shift, and another five worked in the afternoon. The scope of the devastation was so great that this regimen was necessary to prevent the dogs' exhaustion and other health problems. There was a consistency of physical hazards including razor edge metal, fragments of the structure and face of the towers, and cave-ins with multi-story voids below. Each team worked with a "safety person." It was crucial to have an additional pair of hands and eyes to protect the dog from unstable surfaces, and to assist the dog in reaching otherwise inaccessible portions of the site.

Both people were dog handlers, which meant that one of their dogs was left behind to rest, while they worked the other dog. By noon, the handler that had worked his dog in the morning would rest his dog, and become the "safety person" for a new team. During rest breaks, the veterinarians and vet techs who had volunteered to care for the dogs, would flush their eyes and, when necessary, hydrate them using an IV.

There was a central command post, where the teams were directed to report to the battalion chiefs who instructed them where they were needed. The "bucket brigades" were made up of lines of people passing buckets of debris, sometimes removed by hand. Many times Csontos would hear shouts of "dog, dog, dog." He would report to that spot with Odin with the hope there would be a find. Odin alerts by pawing the ground, sitting, and looking to Csontos for his toy. His reward for a find is a game of "tug of war" with his rubber "kong on a rope" toy.

An ironworker requested a dog to search a particular area. They proceeded into a hole with a drop of about five stories. According to Csontos, "It looked as if the entire street had fallen in." It was a confirmation to Csontos of the magnitude of the disaster. The risk to both human and canine was so great they were forced to turn back. "The pain of knowing there might be someone trapped alive down there and not being able to get to them, was unbearable," said Csontos.

Three to four days into the search, they found Odin alerting to a pile of rubble. Csontos crawled in on his knees and uncovered a fireman's glove with a name on it, and a cache of Scott air-packs with severed hoses (that had been worn on their backs or carried). When he found yet another glove, twenty-five firefighters joined in the search. They found face-masks, pieces of helmets, and finally, victims. Odin had enabled the firefighters to find more of their own and the search continued. There was always the hope of making one more recovery providing closure for yet another family.

As they left the site at the end of the day, they walked past hundreds of people who lined the streets holding signs that read "You Are Heroes" and "Thank You" while others waved the American flag: "Why does it take a tragedy to bring people together?" questioned Csontos.

He feels he did what he was trained to do. "The heroes were those who perished; the firefighters, police officers and civilians who went back into those buildings to save lives."

Odin has become a dedicated and loyal team player. His reactions are reliable and instinctive. It is these characteristics that make for a successful team and underscores the need for these unique patrol/ search and rescue dogs.

Photo courtesy of Connecticut State Police

Jutt/Trooper Slonski

Jutt/Trooper Slonski

Connecticut State Police Trooper First Class Kevin Slonski and his canine partner Jutt were one of the teams at Ground Zero. Jutt is a nine-year-old male German shepherd patrol/search and rescue dog.

It was difficult to perceive that pile of debris, several stories high, had been a building. The scene, physically and psychologically, swallowed you up. You found yourself standing in the middle of a giant gaping hole.

Trooper Slonski knew this would be different from any investigation they experienced. There was no preparation for anything of this magnitude. Once they came up with a plan of action, they got down to business. According to Slonski, "Our training kicks in and you do your job."

They had arrived at Ground Zero in the early morning hours, and waited for the battalion chiefs to decide which areas were to be searched. While waiting, Jutt sniffed, scratched at the ground and sat, his trained alert. This had been a well-traveled area by all of the rescue and iron workers. Upon further investigation, Slonski made a recovery directly where Jutt sat. Firefighters joined in the search only to make an additional recovery. It was agreed that were it not for Jutt, the recovery would never have been made. Jutt was able to provide closure for one more family.

Jutt, at the age of nine, sometimes looked fragile. He struggled to get from girder to girder. At one point, he hit his abdomen and began to urinate blood. It turned out that he had broken some blood vessels, was put on medication and made to rest. Jutt resisted, for he was driven to get back to work. The carnage at the World Trade Center site pushed Jutt's abilities to the limit. As Slonski watched Jutt struggle with his gait, he realized it was time for a "changing of the guard." Slonski looks back on their five-year partnership with pride. It includes two life-saving medals.

Slonski carries his experience at the World Trade Center with him daily. He feels for all of the innocent people who lost their lives. He is very connected to the World War II generation and never thought that anything of this magnitude could be wrought upon us in our United States. What makes it even more difficult for him to grasp is the senselessness of it; the fact that this was a deliberate act of violence against the innocent.

Jutt has had a great career. His play drive, social skills, love for people, and most of all, his good heart and soul, have made him one of the greatest search and rescue dogs with the Connecticut State Police K-9 unit. He will be instrumental in training Zubie, the next generation of search and rescue dogs.

Thunder/Trooper Logiodice

This was the first search and rescue mission for Thunder, a three-and-a-half-year-old German shepherd. He was primarily a patrol dog, who had been "cross-trained" for search and rescue work, but had no experience under his belt.

He was at Ground Zero. It was 5:30 A.M. on 12 September 2001, and within ten minutes he had acclimated himself to the noise, people, and surroundings, enabling him to get into his mode and start giving indications to his handler, Connecticut State Police Trooper First Class William Logiodice.

As a patrol dog he is trained to track people by a particular human scent. That human scent is nine times out of ten a "live" scent. When they do search and rescue work, they are relying on Thunder to find any human scent, including the odor of decomposition. There were many finds that day and in the following days.

When Thunder alerts, he looks back at Trooper Logiodice with such intensity, he feels as if the dog's head will snap. Thunder's focus increases as he gets close to the scent. Thunder is at his best when working alongside Logiodice. For him to be able to move away from him for any length of time and remain focused on his work, is a tribute to his dedication and training.

The vast search area at Ground Zero required Thunder to work off leash. Logiodice was concerned about the hazards of portions of the site. There were moments when Logiodice felt the ground to be so very unstable, he would "hand" or pass his dog to the next handler, or abort the mission, and call Thunder back. Thunder's safety always came first.

Logiodice comments, "To walk into that scene and witness the kind of utter destruction one could never possibly imagine, and then see the lines of policemen and firemen removing the remains of two 110-story buildings, one five-gallon bucket at a time, is a sight you can never forget. There would be twenty lines at a time, removing debris." When he would return the next day for his shift, he would be amazed at the amount of debris that had been removed in this manner.

Their department is cross-training more dogs to do patrol and search and rescue work. The use of these dogs is increasing, along with the awareness of their capabilities in this post 9/11 era.

SPECIAL OPERATIONS DIVISION OF THE WESTCHESTER COUNTY POLICE

Pretzel/Officer Langford

He had been dealing drugs for a long time, but covered his tracks so meticulously he was difficult to apprehend. The Westchester County Police Department eventually had enough information to arrest him and then proceeded to build their case. His car had been impounded and searched without success. Pretzel, a three-year-old, black Labrador retriever, and her partner Police Officer Daniel Langford, was asked to conduct a search. Pretzel searched the perimeter and found nothing. Once inside the car, she immediately alerted to the center console. Officer Langford's search revealed a few seeds of marijuana in the base of the center console. A seed is the size of the head of a pin. It was amazing that Pretzel could find such a small quantity of the drug, but it was enough to incriminate the owner.

They did their first search in January of 2001. They have done many since then. Their narcotics unit raided a residence in Cortlandt, New York. Pretzel alerted on three separate locations: a file cabinet contained cocaine, a dresser drawer contained heroin, and a small package of marijuana was found on the floor. In all there were forty decks of heroin, and several ounces of cocaine and crack, making this a substantial find.

When officers stop cars for traffic violations, they may impound the car, if they have reasonable suspicions that there are narcotics in the vehicle. The Supreme Court has ruled "the air is free." A dog sniff is less intrusive than a physical search. When Pretzel is called in, she will run the exterior of the car. If she alerts, this constitutes probable cause, thereby giving the officers permission to search the inside.

Pretzel was almost two years of age when she was released from the Guiding Eyes for the Blind program. She was too high energy for a guide dog career. High-energy dogs, dogs that put their noses into things and search, and dogs who want to fetch the ball and keep it have the kind of qualities that make a great detection K-9.

Photo courtesy of Westchester County Police Department.

Amy/Detective Outhouse

Amy/Detective Outhouse

Amy, a yellow female Labrador retriever, bomb detection canine, worked the President Clinton detail. Her job was to check the airports and his home in Chappaqua, New York, before he arrived and while he was in residence. She would inspect the hangar at the airport and the motorcade.

Detective Robert Outhouse, Westchester County Police Bomb Squad Canine Handler is Amy's handler. In addition to the Clinton detail, they have covered several dignitary-protection details, including Presidents Ford, Carter and Bush. At the Goodwill Games on Long Island, New York, Amy worked alongside the Nassau County Bomb Squad. On one of his visits to the United States, Britain's former Prime Minister John Majors played with Amy, after she completed a search of his meeting place.

This police K-9 team also provides security for many public events. The Westchester County Center is swept regularly prior to all high school graduations. According to Outhouse "it is fabulous to watch these dogs work a room. Suddenly you see their heads snap back, they catch an odor, they sniff it and sit to signal a find. Amy is a tornado when she works."

Photo courtesy of Westchester County Police Department.

Brandt/Detective Gray

Brandt/Detective Gray

Detective Don Gray of the Westchester County Police Bomb Squad will never forget what he saw during a trip to the World Trade Center, when he responded to the terrorist attack in 1993.

It was in that year, when this bustling financial mecca had first been attacked. There was extensive destruction with 2,500 tons of rubble, hundreds of demolished cars and six deaths.

Gray is among six county police officers trained to prevent such a disaster from occurring in Westchester. Squad members are reluctant to discuss their response procedures, but they've got some of the most sophisticated detection and removal equipment in the world. Brandt, a seven-year-old, yellow Labrador retriever is an important part of this team. He was originally trained as a Guiding Eyes guide dog but was released because he was easily distracted. However, he becomes completely focused as a detection dog.

While responding to some 200 incidents a year, the Westchester County Bomb Squad has safely removed industrial chemicals, fireworks and munitions from various locations throughout Westchester County. When President Clinton moved to Chappaqua, New York, the Westchester County Police Bomb Squad assumed a major responsibility. Brandt, along with Detective Gray had to search every piece of luggage before it went on Air Force One.

With the anniversaries of Oklahoma City, Waco and Columbine, there is always a heightened awareness among the school administrations. Media coverage seems to spawn much copycat activity. There was a rash of bomb threats at several local Westchester schools.

Detective Gray and Brandt conducted a thorough sweep to be sure the buildings were safe. These dogs save many man hours searching lockers one by one. Their reputation for competence is well earned. A search that would otherwise take a day can be accomplished in a matter of hours.

The department has great respect for the abilities of these dogs and their importance in the success of their work.

Pete Major has trained all of the Westchester County Police Bomb Squad dogs and handlers. He has also trained K-9 handler teams for private industry. One such client is the New York Stock Exchange, which employs several teams providing continuous sweeps twenty-four hours a day, seven days a week, 365 days a year.

In 1982, he retired from the New York Police Department where he had trained explosive detection canines for ten years. He began his own canine training company in Putnam County, New York. It was then that he formed a relationship with Guiding Eyes for the Blind. He finds their dogs to be intelligent, stable, strong and perceptive. Pups with high energy and motivation, curiosity, and who respond well to food reward, make better detection dogs. Pete finds Guiding Eyes dogs great to work with. They continue to be in a learning mode, so training them is not difficult.

What makes Pete's dogs excel at what they do is the consistency in their training. The old techniques still work. The thrill is there when he begins to train a new dog and realizes the success of his efforts.

Photo courtesy of New Jersey Task Force One.

Piper/Whynman

NEW JERSEY TASK FORCE ONE

Piper/Whynman

The world had changed forever that beautiful, clear, September morning, less than two years into the new millennium. It was like a bad dream. It couldn't be real, but it was and we were all living in the moment that it was happening. Its scope was incomprehensible. There was nothing to compare it to.

Rescue assistance was being offered from around the world. The New York Governor's Office called the New Jersey Office of Emergency Management. "We need search and rescue teams, and we need them now."

New Jersey Task Force One, an elite disaster response team was immediately dispatched and was one of the first to join the NYFD and NYPD at the site. Sonny Whynman and his ninety-five-pound, six-year-old, black German shepherd search and rescue dog Piper began what would be ten exhausting, and emotionally wrenching days. There were moments of fear and moments of celebration, punctuated by long periods of frustration and sadness. The satisfaction of being there and Piper's magnificent performance will be with Sonny for the rest of his life.

Nothing could have prepared Sonny and Piper for the sixteen-acre mountain of white dust-covered debris with scattered valleys and shafts, many hidden, some exceeding fifty feet in depth. There were sharp, slippery and inclined surfaces. The sheer number of rescue workers that were present at the site further complicated the physical condition by making it difficult for Piper to navigate.

Sonny removed Piper's collar to prevent it from being caught on the sea of protruding objects; and the search began. He ran on twisted steel beams and girders, jutting out at dangerous angles. His bare paws, unprotected to give him better traction, suffered irritation and abrasions. At one point he fell into an unseen crevice with an active fire at its base. Before Sonny could dive into the hole to rescue his partner, his supervisor, Joe Ward, who was serving as back-up to the K-9 team, leaped into the opening and lifted Piper out to his handler. Unfazed by this near disaster, Piper kept working until the end of his shift. On the following day, while searching through the rubble and twisted steel, Piper showed particular interest in an area just beneath him. He started scratching at the rubble, whining and looking back at Sonny. This was not his typical "stand and bark" indication for locating a survivor. He had a stressed expression on his face, and his tail was down. He refused to move. Another team was brought in to confirm the find. This scene was repeated many times, by many dogs throughout the entire area, which came to be known as Ground Zero. It became apparent that this was a search and recover mission, rather than a search and rescue mission.

Four teams worked a twelve-hour shift. There were two dogs on and two dogs off around the clock. Sadness, fatigue and the always present white dust permeated the air, but each find celebrated another family's closure.

The fireman's discovery of a shaft leading down to a cavernous void some fifty feet below presented new hope for survivors. Sonny and Piper responded immediately to their call for a K-9. The area was being scoped with remote cameras. The firemen requested that a dog be harnessed and lowered into the shaft alone to try and locate possible survivors. Sonny offered to join Piper in harness and descend with him into the hole. The firemen felt it was too dangerous for a person. Sonny refused to allow his partner to go alone, saying they would both go or neither would go. Soon after, it was determined that the debris contained no desks, no computers, no file cabinets, only the ubiquitous gray dust that permeated everything. There would be no survivors there. This dangerous operation was called off.

Piper was exhausted at the end of each shift. White dust covered his beautiful black fur and found its way into his mouth and eyes. On one occasion, a firefighter whose eyes were hollowed by exhaustion, asked Sonny if he could hug Piper. As he bent down, he wrapped his arms around the stocky dog, and spoke in a voice barely above a whisper. Moments later, when he stood up, his eyes were sharper and his face had more resolve. The mere presence of the dogs created a sense of strength and calm.

All task force teams, including the K-9's were limited to a maximum of ten days' work at Ground Zero. Sonny was exhausted. Piper's paws were raw and his eyes were red, both requiring treatment. Sonny did not want to leave, for part of himself would always remain there. He reflected on God's master plan and the events that brought him and Piper to this place in time.

Piper, born at the Guiding Eyes for the Blind Canine Development Center in Patterson, New York, was destined to become a guide dog. Because of his extraordinary qualities he was selected as a stud dog to increase the lineage of service dogs with his qualities. At one year of age, a genetic eye problem was diagnosed which disqualified him as a stud. He had no vision in his right eye. He had performed his duties all of those years with only one functioning eye, no depth perception and no peripheral vision on his right side. He was released to Sonny who recognized Piper's potential for search and rescue service despite this considerable handicap. They trained and became certified in wilderness search and rescue with the Ramapo Rescue Dog Association. They were then invited to train with and join New Jersey Task Force One for urban search and rescue. This training included dealing with collapsed buildings.

New Jersey Task Force One is an elite urban disaster response team consisting of about 150 doctors, paramedics, structural engineers, rescue specialists, technical search specialists with leading technology, and twelve K-9 search and rescue dog and handler teams. Piper's training included locating survivors buried below rubble. He sits in front of the find and barks to get his reward—a game of tug-of-war. In practice events with a dummy,

Piper has been known to demonstrate his enormous strength by pulling the "victim" out of the debris to insure his instant reward.

Sonny Whynman was a supervisor and high school English teacher in the New York City school system. He would have told you that "that is what I do." Working with Piper in search and rescue is "what I am." He has been a volunteer at Guiding Eyes for the Blind and has raised one German shepherd for their guide dog program. They asked Sonny to harbor Piper when he was in the stud program, and released Piper to him for search and rescue work when his eye problem was discovered.

Sonny is one of those exceptional people who dedicate themselves to helping others. Piper is his partner and best friend. Together they make our world a better place.

CONNECTICUT STATE POLICE NARCOTICS TASK FORCE, EASTERN DIVISION

Oak/Trooper Bardelli

Connecticut State Trooper Bob Bardelli and his drug detection dog Oak were called in to search a residence for illegal drugs. When they reached the garage, with a fourteen-foot-high ceiling, they found boxes stacked halfway to the ceiling. This did not look particularly suspicious—but Oak's keen nose picked up something. She worked her way to the top of the boxes, and stuck her nose straight up in the air. Trooper Bardelli opened and inspected each and every box and found no drugs, only to have Oak climb right back up to the top of the boxes, and again put her nose straight up in the air. Bardelli moved the boxes, found a ladder and climbed to inspect the ceiling. It took him a full five minutes to find a can of raw cocaine cleverly concealed in the roof construction. Without Oak they would never have made this find so high off the ground.

Trooper Bardelli and Oak, a small, black Lab, are assigned to the Connecticut State Police Narcotics Task Force, Eastern division. They work hand-in-hand with federal agencies, such as FBI, DEA, immigration, customs and other agencies.

It took six weeks to have Oak imprinted to the scent of narcotics. Following this training, they went to school for another six weeks to teach Oak how to communicate her find. Oak's body language tells Trooper Bardelli what scent she has found. To Oak, seeking drugs is a game and she is rewarded with food each time she makes a find. They have been on the road together since December of 1997.

Most of their time is spent searching sites suspected of harboring drugs. Standard procedure is for Oak to wait in the van, while the house is secured, and deemed safe for her to enter. Once Trooper Bardelli brings Oak into the house, she becomes the pilot, thoroughly searching every space and piece of furniture. They investigate as few as two to as many as ten houses, a week. They also assist other police departments throughout Connecticut and portions of Massachusetts. The battle to eliminate the sale and use of illegal drugs keeps them very busy.

Soon after they started working together as a team, Oak and Bardelli entered a bar. Oak alerted to a group of men who were gathered around a pool table. Bardelli knew by her reaction that she had found an illegal substance.She went right up to the pocket of a young man, sat, put her nose to the item, and looked at Bardelli. This is her standard routine and alert. Bardelli pulled a package of cigarettes out of the man's pocket, emptied its contents on the pool table, only to find three bags of heroin. Oak can smell the slightest traces of narcotics. Drug dealers have a justified fear of detection dogs. The police officer must always be on the alert to protect his teammate.

Most money in circulation is tainted with drugs, so Oak will hit on 95% of money found in pockets at search scenes. She has been known to embarrass fellow police officers by checking out their pockets.

Federal Express reported a suspicious package. It had no return address, and a fictitious sender. After smelling it just once, Oak gave an alert. Narcotics dogs have contributed to the seizure of thousands of pounds of marijuana through the mail. Most drug detections could not have been accomplished without them.

Reno/Trooper Wynn

The Stamford, Connecticut Narcotics and Vice Unit had search warrants to conduct a sweep of city bars. This search was led by Trooper First Class Michael Wynn and his K-9 partner Reno, a five-year-old, black Labrador retriever. Their target was to search several downtown bars in Stamford.

At the first bar, Reno pulled Wynn into the women's room and alerted to the waste basket, where Wynn found drug paraphernalia. Reno also alerted to two of the seven people sitting at the bar. Following a search, narcotics were found in their possession. They moved behind the bar where Reno searched through a bunch of old beer bottles. He alerted to a case of beer. At the bottom of the box, Wynn found twenty bags of crack-cocaine. On their way to the cellar, Reno started sniffing intently at the riser on the landing area of the staircase. Behind the carpet was a small bag of crack cocaine. He also alerted to an adjacent wall. A portion of the wall was removed, resulting in the discovery of several additional ounces of cocaine.

Trooper Wynn got a tip that a student at a school in Weston, Connecticut was dealing drugs from his car. Reno alerted to the outside of a car parked in the school parking lot. Permission was granted for them to enter the car. Reno alerted and located about five and a half ounces of marijuana. The drugs were found in the fuse box panel of the car. This resulted in an arrest for possession of and dealing drugs.

Narcotics dealers often keep their money and drugs in safes, generally buried deep in closets. Reno will alert to the residue in the seams of the safe. When Reno enters a closet he will jump up, curling his paws so they don't touch anything. He can hold his weight four to five feet off the ground while he sniffs the clothing.

According to Trooper Wynn, "This amazing ability of the dog has vastly increased the efficiency of the police department." Wynn feels he has the best job in the world.

Blossom/Detective Threlfall

Police departments are progressing with the times by utilizing high-tech type resources such as DNA and computers. However, in the Statewide Narcotics Task Force for the Connecticut State Police Department, they still resort to what has worked over the years: the use of dogs to aid them in their investigations. No technical advances can match the K-9's detection ability.

Statewide Narcotics had seized a vehicle that was brought to a common meeting location where approximately 100 officers from that unit assembled. They ordered a "canine sniff" of the vehicle. Blossom, a small, black, narcotics detection Labrador retriever, was called in to perform this task. In her perimeter search, she alerted to two hidden compartments.

From the inside she pinpointed an exact location where she uncovered over $50,000 in US currency in addition to residue amounts of cocaine. She was searching for the cocaine; the money tainted with traces of cocaine was a bonus find.

They conducted an investigation at Bradley Airport in Connecticut. On their way to the scene, Detective John Threlfall was walking Blossom alongside carts piled high with baggage. She suddenly did a back flip to get to a piece of luggage located at the top of the cart, and alerted. They seized sixty-eight pounds of marijuana. Ironically, they were at the airport investigating another case when Blossom made this find.

Blossom has approached people at the airport without being asked to target anyone specifically, and has alerted to them. Threlfall, a plainclothes detective, has to act on this alert by advising

47

the person that Blossom is a narcotics dog and has alerted to them. He always requests their cooperation.

Before the department began using dogs, police officers conducting a search had been known to do a "hand search," often overlooking well concealed drugs. Narcotics can't be hidden from the nose of a trained, drug detection K-9.

When you stop a car, search an airport, or look for a missing or wanted person and that dog is successful, they have made the day. K-9's search cargo-type facilities, airports and shipping terminals, package terminals and any place where there is movement of people and packages.

These dogs are bred and trained by Guiding Eyes for the Blind, for the particular attributes that make good detection dogs: tremendous energy, drive, ability to focus, and not being easily distracted. When police handlers evaluate a dog, they are looking for a dog with a keen nose. The dog must exhibit interest and curiosity. When it comes to size, smaller is better because they can access tight spaces.

Typical training for handlers and K-9's include practical exercises such as searches of vehicles, packages and suitcases, warehouses and postal facilities. At the end of the training period, the forensic chemist gives the dogs the odor recognition test, using a training wheel. A training wheel is made up of two pieces of two-by-fours that are eight feet in length. They are bolted together at the center and placed on a pivot, enabling it to swivel. A gallon can is attached to each end of the two-by-four. Three of the cans contain distracting odors such as food, or perfume. The fourth can is the "hot" can and contains the odor the dog is being trained to find. The dog is told to "seek" and must properly alert to the trained odors. It is a passive alert, where the dog sits and is then rewarded with food. The narcotics dogs are trained to alert to marijuana, cocaine, heroin, methamphetamine, and ecstasy.

As a result of September 11, there will be an considerable increase in the utilization of detection dogs. To thwart acts of terrorism, Guiding Eyes for the Blind is breeding and raising future K-9 "soldiers" who will help protect us during these uncertain times.

FBI

Atwood/Officer Gaines

My name is Atwood. I am a three-year-old, black Labrador retriever. I am one of three explosive detection canines at FBI Headquarters. Michael Gaines, my handler and trainer, and I have been a team for the last several years.

I spent sixteen weeks in training. Michael joined me on the sixth week and we trained together for the last ten. I learned to detect 19,000 different components that make up explosives. Training took place in Front Royal, Virginia. My training class consisted of thirteen dogs, all of whom were trained by the ATF. There were seven Polish officers training canines to return to Poland. Interpreters were needed to assist them.

I love my job with the FBI. We work with special agents from different units, and do "agency training" on federal, county, state and local levels. This includes the Secret Service, Federal Protection Service, Pentagon police and the military. We conduct our training sessions at Union Station, the Kennedy Center, warehouses, airports, vehicles, lockers and classrooms. Using search warrants, we do "pre-search" for weapons at residences.

When President Bush comes to visit FBI Headquarters, specific areas must be cleared, including the route into the building. His motorcade drives into the basement where we do a sweep of the vehicles. We work alongside the Secret Service canines.

Since the September 11 terrorist attack, we have been very busy. One of our first jobs was to check a warehouse that received all the shipments that came to FBI Headquarters prior to the eleventh, including the building perimeter, to insure there were no planted explosives. We had to check every vehicle that entered the FBI parking garage. Everything was under suspicion.

The city of Washington, D.C. shut down following the attack. People abandoned their vehicles as they left the city. The press arrived in droves. Their packages, video cameras and personal belongings were lined up on the street to be checked.

Michael and I are busier than ever. Everyone seems to be more vigilant, with security having been tightened. We train daily so that I can be the best that I can, and keep America safe.

Since 1991, Guiding Eyes for the Blind has placed approximately 430 dogs in careers as detection canines with various law enforcement agencies. The majority are Labrador retrievers working overseas as explosive detection dogs under the ATF/State Department's Antiterrorism Assistance Program. Currently, approximately 341 dogs have gone to ATF in the United States and seventeen other countries.

Guiding Eyes for the Blind's dog breeding program is highly sophisticated, producing puppies that are intelligent, strong, stable, perceptive and patient. These are also ideal traits for a guide dog. Frequently, a litter will include dogs with high energy and exceptional curiosity. These traits, which may disqualify them as guide dogs are ideal traits for detection dogs.

Photo courtesy of Louise Schofield.

Mittzy

Mittzy/Schofield

The New York State Police called Louise Schofield and her German shepherd Mittzy, to find a victim presumed to have drowned in the Hudson River. While Louise sat behind Mittzy in the bow of the boat, she began to read her dog.

Each dog has their signature alert as they pick up the scent on the air currents washing over the bow. Some dogs bark and try to jump out of the boat; some lean over the side, often biting at the water; and some lift their noses. Mittzy alerted to a particular spot. Her signature was a bark and a look toward Louise. To confirm her alert, another search and rescue dog joined the search and alerted to the same location. Microscopic bubbles from decomposition rise to the surface and are detected by the dogs. The waters were murky, making it difficult for the divers to see. Three days later, the body appeared exactly where the dogs had alerted. According to Louise, "Your hope is to save lives, but making a recovery eases the family's uncertainty and gives them closure."

Louise worked for Guiding Eyes for the Blind, where she raised and trained guide dogs. She developed an interest in search and rescue dogs and the work they do to save people. When she met Mittzy, a particularly smart and confident German shepherd, who had been donated to Guiding Eyes for the Blind, Louise thought that she had found the perfect search and rescue partner. Louise began to spend a lot of time with Mittzy, playing ball with her and taking her for automobile rides. They became inseparable. Louise decided to adopt her. Mittzy had the intensity, the drive and the temperament to focus for long periods of time. She had all the traits necessary for a search and rescue dog.

Mittzy and Louise trained together for a year and a half, with the Ramapo Rescue Dog Association. The longer they worked together, the stronger the bond between them grew. Mittzy searched an area by making a "pass," then looked at Louise. Louise signaled to her and the ballet between them began. When she had a find, she would look to Louise, bark and was rewarded with an enthusiastic play session. It was beautiful to watch her develop her skills.

Mittzy and Louise learned to trust each other. Their strength lies in their togetherness. They share a love and excitement for the work they do. It is gratifying to them to know they help people who are lost and in danger. They are lifesavers in the truest sense of the word.

Photo courtesy of Teresa S. Scripture/Guiding Eyes for the Blind.

THERAPY DOGS

Pier 94 located on the bay at 55th Street in Manhattan, was bustling with activity. It was set up as the family service center to support the families of the victims in the aftermath of the September 11 attack. Fragmented families came to find loved ones, unable to accept their catastrophic loss. Many came to begin the painful task of paperwork. Others came because they no longer had jobs.

There were men of the cloth, representing all religions. Cubicles were set up by many of the businesses that had been at the World Trade Center. One could find people from all walks of life; infants, children of all ages, adults and seniors. There was a message wall, the one we all saw on television, carrying photos, messages, trinkets and mementos. The bottom of the entire wall was lined with teddy bears, stacked shoulder to shoulder.

Weaving their way through this crowd of humanity that was dominated by an aura of sadness, loss and emotional pain, were four dogs, and their handlers. Each of these Labrador retrievers wore a cape announcing "Pet Me I'm A Therapy Dog."

Maura Cornish and her dog Pecan, a four-year-old black female Labrador retriever, were there to participate in "grief therapy." As they walked around, people stopped to talk to them. Comfort sounded in people's voices with comments like, "I just needed a lick," or, "The dogs are here." Each team was made up of two people and one dog. There was the handler, and another person, whose job it was to get an overview of the situation. Often the only conversation heard was between people and the dog. On one of their "pass throughs," Maura was told there was a woman who needed to see a dog. As Maura approached the cubicle where the woman was seated, the woman proceeded to sob, her hands folded in her lap. Pecan automatically leaned over, snuggled into her lap, and began to lick her fingers. As her sobs grew stronger, she opened her hand and extended it to Pecan. Pecan continued to lick her, while leaning close to the woman. No words were said.

They walked to the day care area, where Maura met a little girl who had lost her father in the attack. She had been forced to give her dog up in order to merge her family with another. The child explained to Maura she was "kissed by an angel." The child's sister had been home sick on the eleventh, resulting in her mother's decision not to go to work that day. Her mother also worked at the World Trade Center. In the blink of an eye, she could have lost both parents.

Children flocked to Pecan. They would sit on the floor together, while Pecan licked them. This would elicit smiles, and open the floodgates of conversation. Some of the dogs absorbed the stress of the situation. Pecan would sleep the entire day following a visit to the pier.

Cindy Kosacz, a veterinarian, brought Olympia, her black Lab, to Pier 94. They were there the day of the memorial service at Ground Zero. As the families returned to the "Family Service Center" following the service, the intensity of their emotions could be felt.

A woman in a Red Cross Chaplain's uniform approached Olympia, bent over and pressed her head against Olympia's forehead. Cindy heard her whisper, "You do such good work."

A man was sitting alone waiting to be processed. He looked very sad and detached. He had been watching Olympia, when Cindy asked if she could sit next to him. He nodded. He reached down to pet Olympia, and in a voice filled with pain, said, "You have such beautiful eyes." In that one moment, Cindy knew her reason for being there was to connect this wonderful dog with those who could find peace and comfort in her presence.

Shiloe, a seven-year-old black Labrador retriever is a retired brood dog for Guiding Eyes for the Blind. She and her handler Lisa Cole were at the Children's Center at Pier 94, several weeks after September 11. Shiloe wore her vest decorated with a red, white and blue ribbon and an American flag. They were working with two sisters. The younger of the two, who was about eight, was drawing a detailed picture of Shiloe. It showed her vest, ribbons, flag and even her blue-painted toenails. Lisa asked the child to draw a picture for her to take home. Lisa noticed the dog in the picture had water droplets on her face. Could they have been tears? When she completed the task, the child looked up at Lisa and said, "My Daddy is lost." The child's mother joined them, looked at the picture, and began to cry as she likened the child's artistic ability to her husband's. She gathered up her children, thanked Lisa and hugged Shiloe, as they prepared to leave. The encounter had brought their pain to the surface thereby beginning the healing process.

Ronnie Einhorn, and her six-year-old, male, yellow Lab Lobo visited the Children's Center at Pier 94. Professionals trained to work with children who had experienced trauma were there to assist. Ronnie and Lobo worked with the Red Cross volunteers, who came from all over the country. These volunteers had been away from home for several weeks. They were not only homesick but found themselves in the midst of this tragedy and needed to release their own pent-up emotions. They too needed hugs.

Ronnie and Lobo also worked with those people who had been separated from their dogs due to the September 11 attack. All of them needed to reach out to Lobo for comfort.

These dog/handler teams are members of H.A.R.T. (Human Animal Relational Therapy), a local volunteer group formed by Diane Pennington, to provide animal assisted therapy, animal assisted education and animal assisted activities in a variety of programs.

Pecan, Olympia, Shiloe and Lobo were bred at Guiding Eyes for the Blind. Pecan and Shiloe have been active brood dogs for the past several years. The others were released from the training program, judged as not attaining the demanding level of emotional and physical criteria for a guide dog. The standards for therapy animals and handler teams have been set by the Delta Society, a national organization that tests the teams and offers training for the dog and handler.

Teams who participate in H.A.R.T. programs are required to be registered with the Delta Society and have met their established requirements for animal assisted programs.

Temperament testing is conducted to determine if the dog has the "right stuff" for this kind of work. The dog's body language is read, similar to the evaluations at Guiding Eyes for the Blind. The dogs must have social skills, while becoming accustomed to unusual petting, loud noises, hospital settings, those who have learning disabilities, the developmentally delayed, people in wheelchairs, on crutches or walk with an unusual gait. H.A.R.T. program's eight-week course incorporates many of the basics of the puppy-raising program for Guiding Eyes for the Blind.

Maura works at BOCES, a school in southern Westchester, New York, where there are many wheelchair-bound children. Their disabilities result in involuntary reflexes and funny noises. Their tactile senses have been compromised. Maura has talked Pecan through many a tight grip on her fur. The dogs work with children with eating disorders, phobias, those who injure themselves, suffer from post-traumatic stress, who have cerebral palsy and those who suffer from shaken-baby syndrome.

All of these children have been in psychiatric settings at some point and are trying to get their medications adjusted in order to return to school. Maura describes Pecan as being exceptionally snuggly and cuddly, which accounts for her success in the school setting. If the child can get on the floor, Pecan will climb in their lap. They lie together on the floor and snuggle. If the child is confined to a wheelchair, Pecan will put her feet up on the tray, lean in and snuggle them on the cheek.

Communication flows easily while the children lie on the floor with Pecan. This helps them to learn positive behavioral responses, as opposed to violent ones. They learn that relationships can be built on love and trust rather than fear.

When Maura uses a dog in the classroom setting, the children are amazed that the dog can often have similar emotional issues to deal with. A soft spoken student needed to learn to project her voice in order to make her wants and needs known.

She asked Pecan to perform a task, but Pecan ignored her. Maura asked, "Are you using the appropriate tone and volume of your voice?" Once she repeated the command with strength and conviction, Pecan complied.

Occasionally Maura will bring six-week-old puppies to class, prior to their evaluation for guide dog training. The class watches the body language of the puppies. Are their heads and tails down? Are their bodies tight? A look of anxiety on a puppy's face may be an expression of fear and uncertainty. They analyze what might be causing the puppy's concerns, and relate them to their own emotions. Children who won't speak, who feel they have nothing in common with anyone, always have a dog story to tell. In talking about their dog, they are really talking about themselves. The dog becomes an extension of their emotions, often making it easier for them to focus.

Maura makes routine visits to hospitals, libraries and group home functions. She is teaching Pecan new tricks for therapy work. Maura is impressed with what these dogs are capable of accomplishing, their capacity for love and compassion, and how open and wise they are.

Lisa and Shiloe work at the Incarnation House near Columbia Presbyterian Hospital in New York City. It is a residential facility for children with AIDS and HIV. There was a girl of about ten, who couldn't talk. She made noises to communicate. When Lisa brought Shiloe over to the child, she began to shriek. Lisa was concerned that Shiloe's reaction might reflect the potentially stressful moment. Shiloe looked directly into the child's eyes, her tail wagging at full speed. They seemed to be feeding off each other's energy. At that moment, Lisa took a step back and let Shiloe go to work. Many "working" dogs absorb the stress and become totally exhausted after these experiences, but not Shiloe. She is a rock.

Lisa and Shiloe completed the intense eight-week course for the H.A.R.T. program and passed the Delta Society test. Lisa is training her next pup, Shiloe's offspring, in order to continue her work with the Delta Society.

Ronnie Einhorn and Lobo, along with Cindy and Pecan, visit the Incarnation House on a regular basis. At first, many of the children are frightened by the dogs, but by the time they have had their first encounter, new friendships are created. For some, it is the beginning of a new world of love and compassion.

There was a little boy who had difficulty walking. Lobo stayed close to his side, following and anticipating the boy's pace. When the boy slowed, so did Lobo. When he stopped, Lobo was right there, ready to intercept his fall. The boy was touched that Lobo anticipated his every need. A connection had been made.

Lobo will be accompanying Ronnie to work, where she is a school psychologist. Ronnie is mandated to see children with issues identified by a committee on special education. Some of the issues she deals with are the loss of a parent, and adoption. Many of these children have a desperate need for unconditional love which they find in Lobo.

Vesta was released from Guiding Eyes guide dog training for not having the confidence level required of guide dogs. Veterinarian Cindy Kosacz, her raiser, arranged for her veterinary technician Lisa Kane to adopt her.

Cindy, Lisa, and her teenage daughter Alix, felt that Vesta could play an important role in this family by making a difference in Alix's life. Alix had been in a bicycle accident which resulted in a brainstem injury. Alix spoke in a low tone making it difficult to understand her. She learned to sign. Alix, whose ability to swallow has been compromised due to her injury, was choking. Vesta proceeded to run up and down the stairs repeatedly, alerting Lisa to the fact that something was wrong. Lisa arrived in time to save her child.

When Alix has an occasional seizure, Vesta is right there to comfort her. At the onset of a seizure, Vesta goes over to Alix, puts her head in her lap or lies alongside her if she is on the floor. She waits there for as long as it takes for the seizure to subside. Once it passes, Vesta teases Alix with a toy, encouraging her to grab it and toss it for her to retrieve.

Vesta accompanies Alix to many family functions. Her presence encourages wary children to approach and interact with her.

Vesta may not have been trained as an assistance dog, but her breeding and training have enabled her to connect with Alix, and improve the quality of her life.

GUIDE DOGS

Iris

One night Caren's mom was awakened by a wet nose pushing against her arm. In a daze she put on her robe thinking this must be an emergency bathroom call. Slowly realizing that Iris must not have been able to wake Caren up, Caren's mom took Iris to the back door to let her out. Iris wouldn't budge. When her thoughts cleared she recalled that Iris, a yellow Lab, rarely came upstairs, for she was always by Caren's side. Iris kept walking toward the door to Caren's apartment, which was downstairs in the same house. Iris was trying to tell her something, and wouldn't take no for an answer. Caren's mom got the message that something was seriously wrong.

They found Caren lying unconscious on the floor. Iris had glued herself to Caren while her mother called 911. When the ambulance arrived, Iris jumped into the ambulance refusing to be left behind and accompanied Caren to Albany Medical Center. Once the ambulance arrived at the hospital, Iris, being very protective of Caren, planted herself on the gurney which was holding Caren's stretcher as it was wheeled in. A patient commented that she didn't know that AMC was now treating dogs! While at the hospital, Iris was able to relax, sensing that Caren was safe. Caren had been a diabetic since the age of four. Her blood sugar had dropped to an undetectable level, causing unconsciousness. Caren's condition was stabilized while Iris was given the comforts of home: a blanket and a cookie.

Caren is a stand-up comic. She travels three hours by bus into Manhattan, with her guide dog, Iris, to perform and take acting classes. Iris guides her to the stage steps and lies at her feet while she performs.

Iris saved Caren's life. Besides her wonderful husband and daughter, Iris has been the best thing that has happened to her.

Photo courtesy of Dr. Michael Scollard.

Kyack/Michael Moore

Kyack

It was one of those acute intersections in Manhattan, resulting in poor driver visibility. The driver of the car never saw them. As the car swung around the curb in front of them, Kyack acted instinctively and pulled Michael out of the way, preventing a tragic accident. The car came so close to Michael that he felt the rush of air as it passed. The incident made him realize how much in harmony he was with his dog, and what an important role he played in his life.

Michael Moore had been a theatrical costume designer. He lived in Manhattan for ten years. Michael was an assistant designer for off-Broadway productions and regional theatre. He was the wardrobe manager for Tyne Daly's one-woman show, and wardrobe supervisor for the Macy's Thanksgiving Day Parade in 1998. He had been looking forward to graduate school to earn his master's degree. He had earned a full scholarship to the Cincinnatti Conservatory of Music, with an emphasis in costume design for opera.

Michael had been a diabetic since the age of seven. When his eyesight began fading as a young adult, he went to the eye doctor for a new prescription for glasses. He was advised that his problem was much more severe. He was referred to a retina specialist at the New York Eye and Ear Hospital, who diagnosed him with diabetic retinopathy. Months of laser surgery were unsuccessful in saving his vision. When he realized he was going blind, and would be unable to pursue his profession, he was overcome by despair.

Michael received a great deal of encouragement and support from friends and family. Upon making the decision to get a guide dog, he submitted an application to Guiding Eyes for the Blind, and was accepted into the program shortly thereafter. Never having had a dog, he was terrified at the thought of being responsible for a living being.

During training, the students were told the name and sex of their dog, and were asked to return to their rooms to wait. Michael explains, "It was like waiting for the arrival of a baby. It must be the same kind of anticipation and joy." He was called back to the lounge. Shortly after he was seated, he heard the doors open. Although the room was carpeted, he could still hear the pitter patter of paws. Once this happy and muscular dog, named Kyack, licked Michael's face, all fears and concerns disappeared. He was instantly in love with him.

Now that Kyack was an integral part of his life, he was able to consider other career paths. What had been despair gave way to hope for a new future.

Kyack, along with the support of family, friends and Guiding Eyes for the Blind, gave Michael the courage and freedom to attend and graduate from Roger Williams University of Law in Bristol, Rhode Island. Having accomplished this goal has created new opportunities for Michael. His future, a bright one, shines like a marquee on Broadway.

 Trumpet
Soloist

Photo courtesy of Guiding Eyes for the Blind.

Guthrie/Stacy Blair

73

Guthrie

Stacy, an international trumpet soloist, has been playing since the age of thirteen. He studied in Paris for a year on a Fullbright Scholarship, after receiving a master's degree in performance at the University of Louisville. He has performed in fifty-two countries. His career was launched after winning the Maurice Andre International Trumpet Competition. That is comparable to a pianist capturing the Van Cliburn Competition. His repertoire includes more than 140 trumpet concertos. He has performed in concert with the Tel Aviv Symphony Orchestra, conducted by Leonard Bernstein. *The Music Review* in La-Monde-Paris says of Blair, "The American, Stacy Blair, makes the sound come alive with great fullness; his beautiful technique is a musical discourse with a naturalness which denotes perfect mastery."

Stacy has been blind since his premature birth. The need for additional oxygen damaged his retinas. Ironically, Guthrie, a golden retriever, had not been trained by Guiding Eyes for the Blind to be a "special needs" dog, for Stacy's epilepsy had not been diagnosed until much later.

One evening when Stacy was standing at the bar of a restaurant with friends, waiting to be seated, Guthrie sensed a seizure coming on. He nudged Stacey and began to drag him through the restaurant toward the door leading to the street. Stacy was puzzled for this was unusual behavior for Guthrie. Once outside, Guthrie pushed Stacy to the ground. Moments later it was clear to Stacy that he was about to have an epileptic seizure. A seizure can cause immediate loss of consciousness with the risk of serious injury. How does one explain the fact that a dog can anticipate a seizure? Stacy describes the "aura" that occurs. His ears begin to ring, he gets a hot flash, and he senses the smell of vanilla. Guthrie seems to sense these changes before Stacy does. If Stacy's seizure takes the form of a daze, Guthrie will put his head on Stacy's lap until it passes. If the seizure forces Stacy to the floor, Guthrie will lie beside him with his head on Stacy's chest.

Another passion in Stacy's life is bowling. He belongs to a regular league, carries a 142 average, and has won a "Century" award for bowling a 242. Guthrie loves going to the bowling center, for he gets to shed his harness and act like a big puppy. Stacy lines up by feeling the machine and moves the necessary number of inches. After his first shot, his friends tell him what he has left and he adjusts his position to complete the spare. He listens for the machine to tell him when his ball returns. Using his sense of touch he can recover his ball, which has a distinctive feel.

Stacy does much to help others. Guthrie accompanies Stacy when he makes appearances at elementary schools to teach the children that blindness does not have to be limiting. His cookbook for the blind, entitled *Cooking Without Looking*, is on tape. He raises money for Guiding Eyes for the Blind, is a consultant and spokesman for Make A Wish Foundation, and does work for the Epilepsy Foundation of America.

Guthrie is always by his side: when he travels, performs and enjoys life. According to Stacy, "He is the closest thing to heaven."

Photo courtesy of Guiding Eyes for the Blind.

Kim/Vincente A. Paratore

Kim

The stroke damaged his optic nerve leaving him blind in one eye and with little vision in the other. This loss of vision was especially devastating since painting was not only his profession, but an all-consuming passion. It was his life.

As he recuperated from his stroke in the hospital, Vincente's thoughts brought him back to his childhood. His father died when he was eleven, creating the need for Vincente and his sister to find work. They designed window displays for department stores. It was a turning point in his life when he realized how much he loved the world of art.

Lying in his hospital bed, Vincente had a vision. It took the form of an angel, wrapped in soft and gentle light, giving him a sense of calm. She made him aware of the love he had for his painting. After he spoke to the angel, he realized his art wasn't about his eyes, but his soul. He was inspired to paint once more.

Vincente made a conscious decision to live and called Guiding Eyes for the Blind, to begin the process of getting a guide dog. Vincente enjoyed every moment of his three weeks at guide dog school. In appreciation, he cooked a gourmet dinner for everyone. When Vincente met his guide dog Kim he was seated in the center of the room. She jumped right on top of him, covering him with wet kisses. The excitement continued to build when Vincente and Kim began to train together.

He found the warmth of her companionship has changed the way he thinks and paints. Kim has given Vincente a new sense of security and independence. Her temperament is similar to his, making her perfect for him.

77

Vincente has developed a painting technique that allows him to paint by using his sense of touch. He mixes his colors on a table that is lit from below. With the little vision he has, he can discern and manipulate hues. The artist, who for decades painted what he saw with his eyes, now creates beautiful paintings from his reservoir of memories.

Today Vincente lectures at schools and hospitals, inspiring others with his work and his courage. In his native Argentina, Vincente has used his art to draw attention to the plight of people with disabilities, and has been instrumental in making plans to build a school for the disabled. He says, in his beautifully accented English, "I went there and moved a mountain."

Vincente's paintings now reflect his inner confidence and happiness. They are vibrant with color and movement. Not only has he been given a new life through Kim, but in overcoming this devastation, he has become stronger and the experience has enriched his soul. In gratitude he has dedicated his life to giving back to the community.

Photo courtesy of Bill Baskay.

Allan Golabek

Kessler

It was a beautiful day. Allan, his brother and some friends, were on their way to a motorbike rally in upstate New York. They planned to stop for a picnic along the way. They fueled their motorcycles, and pulled out of the gas station single file.

The last thing Allan remembers were the clothes his brother was wearing, the color of his bike and helmet, and his brother waving his arms while yelling "get back, get back." He never saw the car that hit him. Allan was rushed to the hospital where he was treated for a broken femur, and fractured ribs. He required a pin in his knee and hip, and his jaw had to be rebuilt. There were tubes everywhere. Unbeknownst to the medical team working to save Allan, there was a puncture in his aorta. A priest was called in to give Allan his last rites. Allan's mother begged the medical staff not to give up on her son. After an hour and many pints of blood, they located the cause of Allan's bleeding and were able to repair it. In the days that followed, Allan's lungs filled with fluid, he went into cardiac arrest and had a heart attack.

As one problem was solved, Allan's injuries presented the medical team with another. The lack of blood and oxygen to Allan's brain was causing his brain to swell. The swelling was so great it injured the optical nerve which plunged his world into total darkness.

After six weeks in the hospital, Allan entered a rehab facility. That's when reality hit him. He was blind. He fell into a deep depression. He spent four months in rehab. Upon his release he was able to walk with the use of two canes, and spent the first month with his mom. In time, he regained enough strength to return to his own apartment.

Prior to the accident, Allan enjoyed outdoor activities such as white water rafting and canoeing. He was adventurous and always on the go.

One day a friend called to ask Allan to help him build a frame for a canoe. As Allan cut up wood strips to be applied to the boat, his spirits lifted. He felt useful and determined to rid his body of the anti-depressant drugs he had become so dependent upon.

As Allan got stronger and bolder, he felt that the use of canes was limiting his movements. Heeding his Aunt Sally's suggestion that he get a guide dog, Allen filed an application with Guiding Eyes for the Blind.

Wayne, a representative from Guiding Eyes for the Blind came to see Allan. Wayne was very impressed with Allan's work. He watched him measure, sand, cut, fit and glue the pieces to the boat. He knew that he would be a prime candidate for a guide dog.

Allan was paired with a beautiful, black, male Lab named Vulcan. They began to train together. In the middle of a four-way intersection in White Plains, New York, Vulcan froze. He glued himself to Allan's leg and refused to move. When they returned to Guiding Eyes in Yorktown, Vulcan was immediately removed from the program. The only other dog that was available at that time, was Kessler, a three-year-old male black Lab. Allan was given the choice of accepting Kessler or returning for a younger dog and training at a future date. Allan agreed to take Kessler.

When Kessler entered the room, he came bounding over to Allan, licking his face. Allan used his hands to see Kessler. He was stocky and beautiful, but when they retired to Allan's room, Kessler was distant. He was there 100% when it came to working, but kept his affections in check. Melinda, Allan's trainer, asked Allan to be patient.

In time, Kessler came around. "He has become more than a best friend; he's more like a son," says Allan. He got Allan out of bed each morning, forcing him to fight his depression. Allan was determined to function now that he was responsible for Kessler's life.

Allan's friends knew that he needed a physical outlet, so they got him involved with a water ski club. His friends took him "barefooting." A boat pulls you as your bare feet skim across the water. Allan turned out to be a natural. He claims it was because he was so frightened, that he "listened to every instruction like it was his last." He performed so well, he was asked to train with the goal of competing. A local newspaper ran an article on Allan, and the article wound up on the desk of Joel Zeissler, a national water-skiing champion. He called Allan to tell him he was working with a blind water-ski jumper and would like to train Allan at the same time. Joel taught Allan three-event skiing: jumping, skiing, and slalom. Allan entered his first national competition in 1996. He placed second in slalom, and second in jumps. Several years ago, he set two world records in jumping. Allan was part of the National Water Ski Team for the United States and competed in England and Australia.

Allan achieved the goal he had set for himself, and that was to become the number one water skier in the world. Setting these goals and accomplishing them, helped him overcome his depression for good.

The desire not to go back to that painful time keeps Allan moving forward. His accident could have left him paralyzed. He could have lost his leg, or been in a wheelchair. Everything he feels, hears and smells gives him a new appreciation for life.

Through Kessler, Allan has learned how to love and to trust. Once he accepted his blindness, a tremendous weight was lifted off his shoulders. He learned how to turn a negative into a positive. Allan gives back to his community by visiting schools and speaking to children with disabilities. He has Kessler to thank for that, for it is Kessler that gave Allan the strength to face the future.

Photo courtesy of Rivera Family.

Salty/Omar Rivera

Salty

The narrow stairwell was crowded with people. They were pushing and shoving, crying, screaming and praying. A sense of terror permeated the atmosphere. Shards of glass were flying and falling around them, adding to the chunks of debris and pools of water. He heard the crackling of walls and felt floors buckling and then falling apart. Mr. Rivera could feel the acrid smoke and sickening smell of jet fuel fill his lungs. The heat was unbearable.

Omar Eduardo Rivera, a New York resident, was on the seventy-first floor of the World Trade Center north tower when the first of two hijacked planes hit the building on September 11. Mr. Rivera, who is blind, is a senior systems designer for the Port Authority of New York and New Jersey. He was in his office with his guide dog Salty, a four-year-old yellow male Lab, who was lying under his desk at the time of the impact.

Mr. Rivera said he heard an explosion, then silence, followed by the rustling of papers, the crunching of broken glass and the thud of his computer as it hit the floor. The situation was disorienting for Rivera and Salty. He said his prayers amidst the screams of co-workers, and reached for Salty to guide him. Salty responded by following the exodus to the stairway, with Rivera in tow.

In the midst of the noise, heat and chaos of a fleeing crowd, a co-worker offered assistance. As Mr. Rivera took hold of her arm, she led him down the stairs on his right side, while Salty walked on his left. Mr. Rivera was aware of many people passing them. He knew he would be unable to run down the stairs and through all the obstacles like the others, and became resigned to the fact that it was unlikely that he would make it. It was unfair that they should both die in that hell. He hoped that Salty would be able to run down the stairs without him and make it to safety. So he unclipped Salty's lead, ruffled his head, gave him a nudge and ordered him to go ahead.

Mr. Rivera was swept away by the rush of people fleeing down the stairs and found himself alone for several terrifying minutes. He suddenly felt a familiar nudge from down below. Salty, who had not gone far, had returned to his side and guided Mr. Rivera down the remaining flights of stairs and out onto the street. Salty was exhausted after reaching the ground floor an hour and fifteen minutes later. Minutes after they had reached the ground and had gotten to safety, the tower collapsed.

There have been many sleepless nights since the attack. Gone are the routines that once made his life comfortable and familiar.

Mr. Rivera will have to find a new road to travel. However difficult that will be, it will be eased by the knowledge that his best friend and companion, Salty, will be by his side for years to come.

Logan

Logan seemed stressed. He kept placing his head in Walter's lap for a "hug." He was telling Walter that there was something wrong.

Walter Cone, one of many blind people working for the Lighthouse for the Blind in Seattle was on the phone with a customer when the vibrations began. It took all of about ten seconds before he was sure it was an earthquake. Everyone began to scream and run for the exit. Walter advised the people around him to get under their desks and stay there. Taking his own advice he joined his Labrador retriever guide dog Logan, who had been sitting under Walter's desk.

Walter and Logan waited. Everything was moving. There was the thunder of things falling, and the feeling of terror that the desk could collapse. It seemed like an eternity. Then it stopped. The quiet of the moment was brought to a halt by the movement of people. Walter emerged from under his desk. His every step was blocked by debris. Logan, taking it all in stride, walked Walter around the ceiling debris that had fallen and led him out of the building.

Once outside, Walter learned that there were approximately twenty blind and developmentally disabled individuals still inside the building. Ignoring the danger of aftershocks and additional collapses, with Logan leading the way, he re-entered the building guided by the sounds of moaning and calls for help. Walter and Logan found people hiding in rooms on the third floor.

They were injured, confused and frozen in fear. Walter was able to convince them that Logan was with him and could lead them to safety. The group walking hand-in-hand; formed a human chain, while Walter held onto Logan's harness. They picked their way ever so carefully around the rubble and downed wires. Eventually they found their way outside to safety.

Despite the very real risks of the building or portions of the structure collapsing, Walter and Logan made two additional trips into the building to rescue those who remained. Logan took each trip in his stride, remaining cool and calm. He acted like a real trooper.

That night, Walter sent a message to Guiding Eyes to tell them what "his boy" had done. Walter never thought of their actions as being heroic, but was proud of Logan and the confidence his fellow workers had in him.

RAISERS

Karin Skoog

I sat in the room, eyes glued to the television, watching the dog I spent so many months training, as she completed each part of the final test she was asked to perform. My heart filled with a sense of pride when she walked well, or sat on command, or responded well to surprises. With each small triumph, I reveled in knowing it was due to my efforts that she could perform every portion of the test so well. All the numerous hours spent training her, all the seemingly simple exercises repeated over and over, all of my hard work was reflected in the abilities she displayed now.

Despite the extraordinary faith I had in her, my breath caught whenever she faltered or made an error, knowing she could do better and fearing that the mistakes would add up, deeming her unfit to continue in her training as a guide dog. I knew as I listened to the comments and gasps from the other raisers as they watched their dogs, that we all had the same fears.

At last, all the handlers told their dogs to sit, and we waited to hear the final decision, the ultimate decision, a decision that would determine the fate of each dog. I sat there in silence, listening intently for the voice from the television to ring out over the murmurs of the other worried raisers. After the most prolonged few minutes of my life, everyone fell silent when we heard "the voice" start to speak. Every mistake my dog made came flooding rapidly through my mind as I heard the sighs of relief from raisers who heard that their dogs passed. When I thought I couldn't stand it any longer, the voice said, "Lara...passed."

Relief rushed through me. She was in! Maybe, just maybe, the next time I would see her would be at her graduation from the program. I realized I was getting ahead of myself and focused instead on the excitement I felt at seeing her again. I stood at the glass door, watching for her.

When I saw a small, dark shape prance towards the door, my heart gave a little leap, and I stood aside to let my little black dog waltz through. I dropped to my knees and hugged her as she licked every inch of my face. I held her and said, "You did it, Lar! You did it!" She looked up at me, her dark eyes sparkling as she nudged my nose. I laughed and pet her gently, fearing I wouldn't have much time to say good-bye. I wanted to freeze this moment in my memory forever, before she was gone. The excitement was contagious as I watched her dance around, licking every person she could reach. She bounded over to me, and I hugged her and whispered, "Do the best you can." That was all I could expect of her now. I taught her the foundation of what she needed to know. "Are you ready?" the handler asked. I nodded and watched my puppy, the puppy I cared for and loved for over a year, walk out of my life.

Although I wasn't ready to see her go, I was overjoyed to think about the life that lay ahead of her. She had the ability to give someone else an amazing gift—the gift of sight. She turned to look at me, and I smiled. She was still in the early stages of her life. She had so much time left to learn and grow. Just before she turned the corner, I whispered, "I love you, Lar." And then she was gone, gone from my life forever…but not from my heart.

Jennifer Turner

My puppy-raising experience with Guiding Eyes for the Blind began in March of 2003 when I was fifteen years old. For many years I had wanted to love and care for a puppy of my very own. That dream came true when my parents announced that I would be taking classes to learn how to be a volunteer puppy raiser for Guiding Eyes for the Blind.

Attendance at these weekly classes, held by the Cuyahoga Puppy Raising Region, gave me all the tools I needed to be successful. Through the dedicated efforts of the Cuyahoga Region, I learned all about grooming a pup, teaching it commands and good manners, and training it in all kinds of social situations and settings.

After much preparation, the "big day" finally arrived. On June 5, 2003, a black male Labrador retriever named Terence, came bounding into my life. That was the beginning of a year-long adventure that I will never forget.

The first stage of puppy raising was so intense I enlisted the help of my two sisters and my parents. Together, we worked on things like housebreaking, inappropriate chewing, barking, keeping all four paws on the floor and early commands such as sit, down and stay. Soon I was training Terence out in the community, letting him get adjusted to walking on sidewalks while hearing traffic sounds in the background. I also trained him in parking lots, in front of stores, on various stairs and under footings. Daily massages and weekly grooming sessions helped Terence and I create a special bond.

Once Terence received his "Puppy in Pre-training" jacket at ten months of age, the fun really began! His presence in offices and stores really got people's attention. I quickly learned to be more comfortable speaking to total strangers about Terence and Guiding Eyes. I also learned to be assertive with people who wanted to pet and visit with Terence while I was training him.

Terence passed his "In-For-Training" test in August of 2004. He was chosen for the Special Needs Program and was trained for eight months. He was matched with his Canadian partner, Kevin, and graduated in April of 2005. I was able to attend the graduation with my mom and our area coordinator. What an exciting day that was to see my boy all grown up with a very important job! I was so proud of Terence and so happy for him and Kevin.

Guiding Eyes not only gave me puppies to love and to care for, they gave me the opportunity to grow through their various volunteer programs. Puppy sitting for other raisers, helping at classes, and making presentations to expand the Cuyahoga Region of GEB has helped me sharpen my skills. I assist in the recruiting of new raisers, and fund raising. It has also been my privilege to volunteer at their Canine Development Center in Patterson, New York.

I would like to say a sincere thank-you to Guiding Eyes for the Blind for entrusting me with the raising of Terence, Jacobi, Unica and Casper; four friends who have made a difference in my life.

Daniel Swift

It's 5:30 in the morning and I wake up to a whining noise downstairs. I roll out of bed, drag myself down the stairs and see a black ball of fur standing in her kennel, waiting for me to let her out. I open the crate, put a leash on her and pick her up to bring her outside to get busy. After she has done her business, she runs back to me as I praise her in my happy voice. I carry the pup back into the house and I walk over to the counter to grab her soaked breakfast. By now she knows what it means when I lift that silver dish off the counter. So I ask her to sit before I put the dish on the floor. For ten seconds, she plops her bottom down and wags her tail, never taking her eyes off me holding the dish. Then I tell her "Okay" which she knows means she can finally have her breakfast. Little does she know, we will go through this routine two more times today, along with brief obedience lessons, and the exercise she needs to stay healthy. My hope is that this three-month-old puppy, named Dixie, will become the eyes for a visually impaired person, providing independence, friendship and unconditional love.

Guide dog puppy raising has been a significant part of my life for the last ten years. The experiences that come from raising these puppies are things that I will always remember. I have learned many skills through guide dog raising as well as having accomplished many personal goals I set for myself. I have put a lot of time and energy into raising guide dogs and enjoyed every moment.

Since 1996, my family and I have been raising guide dogs. I first found out about guide dog puppy raising through 4-H when I joined as a seven-year-old. My family and I have raised ten dogs through the

Guiding Eyes for the Blind program and I am currently raising our eleventh puppy, Dixie, a black Labrador retriever. I have been the primary raiser for two of these dogs, Wegman and Pierce, and have co-raised two others, Heath and Nutmeg. I have inspired family and friends to become involved in this program.

As an eleven-year-old in sixth grade, I came up with the idea of having a dog sponsored by the school I was attending, Livonia Central. As vice president of the student council that year, I was able to bring the idea of sponsoring a puppy to the student council representatives. It was approved, but we still needed to raise the $750 to donate to Guiding Eyes for the Blind in order to name a puppy after our school. Although the goal was accomplished after I had graduated from sixth grade, my younger brother was able to see this project to completion. Livonia Intermediate School donated $750 to Guiding Eyes for the Blind and my family raised Livonia. The entire Intermediate School was hoping Livonia would become a guide dog. In March of 2003, Livonia graduated with her companion Mary.

My fourth dog, Pierce, was probably the most special in my heart. His low-key personality was nearly an exact match to my own. He always seemed to want to please and he learned quickly. He was an intelligent dog and very responsive to my commands. I enjoyed taking him out into public places because he was so well behaved. I will always remember the bond and great experiences I had with Pierce.

I have come to learn never to underestimate the abilities of these dogs. Last month, I was surprised to learn that Harley, a pup my family raised to become a guide dog, also had the responsibility of detecting seizures in his visually impaired companion. With additional training, he can now alert people who care for his companion's medical condition.

Raising guide dog puppies for the past ten years has been extremely rewarding and has enabled me to always have a pup by my side. Through my involvement with Guiding Eyes for the Blind, I have met and worked with a diverse group of thoughtful and caring people. I have been able to learn, practice, and perfect my dog handling skills and my overall knowledge about dogs. I have also learned about what life is like for visually impaired people and how raising a guide dog for them can have such a positive impact on their lives. In successfully raising a guide dog I am offering a visually impaired person a sense of independence. That gives me a great sense of accomplishment.

Jennifer Stone

I started raising guide dogs when I was nine years old. Together with my family we raised six dogs, and shared all of the work of raising the puppies. When I turned fifteen, I received Erin, my seventh guide dog pup, to raise on my own. Erin was gorgeous and came to me when she was six months old from a previous raiser who could no longer care for her. Her adorable brown puppy eyes and happy-go-lucky personality was all it took for me to fall in love with her. I was responsible for driving Erin to puppy classes, scheduling her evaluations, and socializing her.

For six years prior to receiving Erin, I was very active in my community. I volunteered at fairs and trade shows to promote Guiding Eyes for the Blind. My family and I planned several fund-raisers for Guiding Eyes, and participated in the Guiding Eyes walk-a-thon. With Erin by my side I became an assistant area coordinator, and did presentations at libraries, schools, and nursing homes. These presentations enabled me to inform people about Guiding Eyes for the Blind. I even recruited some families to become puppy raisers. Erin and I made a great team.

Erin made a huge impact on my life. Although I had raised six dogs before her, I don't believe I was ever as close to them as I was to Erin. She taught me patience, understanding, and about unconditional love. I cherish those memories. She touched not just my life, but the lives of so many, including her owner, Linda, whom she safely guides every day. I am very thankful that I was able to experience this opportunity, and hope to share this same experience with my children someday.

Aaron

It is the raiser who provides the emotional foundation and initial training for these wonderful dogs bred by Guiding Eyes for the Blind. Eighteen months of hard work, dedication and love enable these dogs to develop their full potential and go on to become guide or service dogs.

As part of his training, Aaron, a black Labrador retriever, was taken to visit several elementary schools in the Greece, New York area. At one particular school there were 183 third graders in attendance for an assembly. Sandy, Aaron's raiser, was addressing the assembly while Aaron was lying patiently by her side. The children were seated on the floor of the auditorium. Sandy spotted a little girl with braces on her arms and legs, seated about three quarters of the way back. While Sandy was speaking, the child kept sliding herself forward until she was in the front row. Sandy watched as the child hesitantly put her hand out to pet Aaron. She was petting his leg, when suddenly he swung around and planted a big, wet kiss on her face. She grabbed her face and yelled, "He kissed me, he kissed me!"

As the children filed out of the auditorium, a teacher approached Sandy explaining, "You may not realize it, but that little girl rarely speaks." Aaron's amazing sensitivity created a bridge between him and the child.

Sandy Walker, a teacher's aide, had read an article in the local newspaper about the need for raiser families in her area. It occurred to her that she could raise a pup for Guiding Eyes for the Blind, and share the experience with the school children.

Aaron officially started school with Sandy. Aaron began his day with hall duty, where the children greeted him on their way to class.

He then returned to Sandy's office where he played with the children who were waiting to be counseled. Sandy found the children would open up more readily after spending time with Aaron. He visited various classrooms such as the technology class where the noise of the hammers and saws didn't seem to faze him. While Sandy offered assistance, Aaron would lie on the floor or visit with the students.

One day as they were heading down the hall, Sandy noticed that a teacher was questioning six boys who were lined up against the lockers. There had been an incident involving the explosion of a firecracker in the hall. As Aaron walked past the boys, his nose shot up in the air, he zoomed across the hall and went right up to one of the boys. Unbeknownst to everyone, Aaron had identified the culprit responsible for the incident.

The school has used caring for Aaron as a reward for good behavior. Children who have made an effort to improve their discipline problems are given the privilege of walking and feeding him. The student council decided to create a fund-raising event called "Aaron Week." They sold carnations and donated all of the profits to Guiding Eyes for the Blind. "Pennies for Puppies" collected $500.00. The "Aaron Fund" collected several thousand dollars that was proudly donated to Guiding Eyes. With a donation of this magnitude, Arcadia Middle School was given the honor of naming a puppy. Each homeroom submitted a name, with the final selection to be put to a vote. Would it surprise you to learn that the winning name was ARCADIA?

Sandy is prepared to handle the children's separation anxiety when Aaron goes back to Guiding Eyes for guide dog training. Separation can be a painful part of growing up. The children are being taught that Aaron has a destiny to fulfill. The raising of Aaron has been a joint effort. All those involved have been affected by the experience and their attachment to him.

Ramona

Mark was born without eyes. He was terrified of dogs until he met a large black Lab named Ramona in his seventh grade classroom. He became more and more comfortable with Ramona. Eventually Mark asked if he could walk Ramona. Mark picked up Ramona's leash, using the "let's go" command, and off they walked down the hall. As they reached the cafeteria, several students emerged surrounding Mark and Ramona, bombarding him with questions about the dog. Mark was delighted to be considered an expert on the subject.

Maura Cornish, a teacher for the visually impaired, traveled from school to school with Ramona, whom she was raising for Guiding Eyes for the Blind. Mark was a student of Maura's. When he first met Ramona, he was told that she would lie on the floor while he and Maura worked together on math.

Mark reached down to confirm her presence, and ran his hand along her soft fur. He asked Maura, "What's that noise?" The noise was Ramona chewing on a bone filled with peanut butter. Mark remarked that he too loved peanut butter and smiled all through their work session.

Maura conducted an assembly in front of the entire seventh grade. She requested that Mark join her and Ramona on stage. Mark discussed his mobility, his first experience with a cane, and how he used to bump into things. Mark's parents struggled to keep him in a mainstream school. He was the only student in the Braille program, and used adaptive equipment in the classroom.

As for Mark, Ramona has enabled him to move into a more comfortable social situation in school. To his delight, he is no longer the "blind boy" but one of the guys.

RAMONA—written by Mark

Big and strong like a horse.
Licking people like a slippery eel.
Does not bark like an egret.
Stays quietly under the table like grass on the ground.
Walks by my left side like my cane.
Eats peanut butter bone like a seagull.
Ramona is a precious gem.
Wonderful dog.

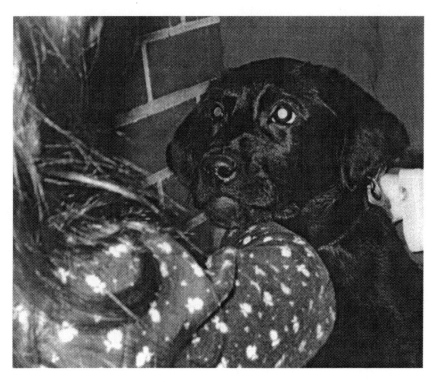

Photo courtesy of Michele Lemis.

Fenway

Fenway

Like a butterfly, eight-year-old Sarah was spreading her wings, preparing to fly. She discovered her love for life and her ability to express her feelings through writing.

Sarah treasured the wonderful memories of the previous year she spent in Michele Lemis's second grade class. The most thrilling part of this experience was the class's participation in raising Dundee, a puppy for Guiding Eyes for the Blind. They learned about giving and receiving love, and teaching Dundee good manners. Sarah's understanding that Dundee was meant to fulfill his special purpose gave her the strength to deal with the pain of separation when he went on to guide dog school.

In the midst of her metamorphosis, tragedy struck. Her father, a policeman, died in a heroic act while protecting the lives of others. Completely devastated, Sarah shut down and withdrew into herself.

Sarah's memories of times past with her dad brought her comfort. She recalled the fun things she did with him. She used to sit on his lap while he sang to her in his rich baritone voice. In the winter they went ice-skating. She loved to hold his hand while he pulled her along. When he let go, off she would skate, using the wall to stop. During the summer he taught her to swim. He would swim beyond her, encouraging Sarah to swim toward him. He pushed her to achieve, which made her proficient at many tasks.

Unable to cope with her heavy heart, she returned to the place where she felt at ease, Ms. Lemis's classroom. Sarah had been deeply touched by the experience of raising Dundee. That was a wonderful time in her life. She needed to rekindle those feelings that tragedy had taken away.

The Dundee program had been so successful that Ms. Lemis decided to raise a new puppy named Fenway, a black, male Labrador retriever. Fenway came to school with her regularly.

Ms. Lemis recognized Sarah's need to heal, and arranged with her third grade teacher to allow her to visit Ms. Lemis's classroom on a regular basis to assist with the younger children.

As Sarah moved around the room helping Ms. Lemis, she never took her eyes off Fenway. He had a way about him that made her feel safe and calm. His eyes were like velvet. He looked at you as if he could see your soul. She found herself drawn to him. She would sit in the back of the room, on a rug, snuggling with Fenway. He loved to lie on his back with his paws up in the air. As she gazed into his eyes, she mouthed the words, "I love you."

Ms. Lemis along with Carol Cutler, co-author and co-educator, created a program for her second grade class entitled Honoring Diversity. She taught the class the importance of Fenway's future as a guide dog. For the chapter on blindness, the children wore blindfolds and learned about Braille. They learned to use their other senses such as taste and smell, and how to eat from a plate without sight, describing the food and its location on the plate.

The school day ended with "schmooze time." This was the time of the day where the children, along with Ms. Lemis, sat in a circle with Fenway at its center. They talked about what they had accomplished that day and shared their feelings on a variety of subjects. As the children stroked his shiny coat, they talked about how he would improve the quality of life for someone in need and his future as a guide dog. They discussed the sadness they would feel when he left them to enter guide dog school. The pain of separation began as Fenway moved closer to that goal. They so very much wanted him to succeed.

One of the classroom projects was the *Fenway Gazette*. This was a student-authored newsletter that included poems, interviews, and progress reports. It gave the students the chance to express their feelings about what it meant to have Fenway in their class. It also served to keep the parents informed and involved in this unique and very rewarding program.

Sarah saw how much Fenway meant to the other children. For John, a student with Down's syndrome, who visited once a week, "Wednesday with Fenway" became the highlight of his week. When John visited Ms. Lemis's classroom, he not only got down on the floor with Fenway, he sometimes crawled into Fenway's crate. He would turn to Fenway and say, "Fenway kiss." That was music to Fenway's ears.

Sarah continued to visit Ms. Lemis's classroom for the rest of that year. The relationship Sarah shared with Fenway released feelings that had been frozen in time. She realized her father had left her with a legacy of love that gave her the courage to follow her dreams. She still dreams of him and will always miss him. By the time the school year came to an end, Sarah was writing once more and had rediscovered her spirit.

Sarah and the other children have started the "letting go" process, as Fenway's "raising days" come to an end. The depth of the children's commitment to Fenway was profound. One second grader wrote:

A Whole New Life
by Kelly Nurge—second grader

He walks on all four legs
He is my only hope
He is my eyes
Don't make fun of me
I'm blind, but I am you.

Fenway has touched the school and the community and has been a bridge in healing Sarah's enormous loss. Both he and the curriculum have taught the students about patience, tolerance, awareness, and sacrifice. Through this program they have come to understand and accept people's differences. They are learning what it is like to give of themselves in order to help others.

This story is dedicated to my granddaughter Sayde.

Olga

Gretchen Schmeider, a raiser from upstate New York, was having separation anxieties as the time approached for her pup Olga to leave for training. Gretchen decided to spend their last night together on the floor with Olga. She dragged her pillow and blankets to the floor by her bed. She held Olga, saying teary goodbyes and eventually cried herself to sleep.

When Gretchen woke up, she found Olga sound asleep in the middle of her bed, while Gretchen's aching bones were a painful reminder of the night she had spent on the hard floor.

RELEASE DOGS

Photo courtesy of Bucklin Family.

Kolina/Kyle

Kolina

Kyle was misdiagnosed. He did not have a learning disability, as originally thought, but Asperger syndrome and Tourette's syndrome, both claiming many autistic mannerisms. "AS" kids are very bright, but socially inept. They want to be a part of the world around them, but because these illnesses make that so difficult to achieve, they become frustrated and depressed.

Kyle had poor language skills. He did not speak voluntarily. His pediatrician felt that Kyle would benefit from having a dog for a pet.

Guiding Eyes for the Blind had just released a black, female Lab named Kolina. Guiding Eyes felt Kolina was very special and should go to a child who really needed her.

Kyle bonded with Kolina immediately. He is silently caring, and does not speak to her except to call her name. He spends the majority of his waking hours with her. When Kyle sleeps, Kolina sleeps beside him. Kolina is his best friend and in times of distress—his comfort.

School is traditionally difficult for Kyle. Since getting Kolina all of that has changed. Kyle is more alert and relaxed since Kolina has become part of his life. He now responds to people coming into a room and someone calling his name. When Kyle comes home from school he takes Kolina upstairs to his room. He spends much of the time by himself, unless he invites you to join him. Theirs is a silent world of love.

The local middle school is raising a black Lab named Aaron. When Kyle and his Mom went to school to meet his teacher, they met Aaron at the door as he greeted the parents and children. Kyle walked in, and stopped dead in his tracks. His face broke into a wide grin, and he headed straight for the dog. He got down on the floor and began a conversation with the principal and vice principal. He said, "I have a dog, her name is Kolina. We got her in May. Why is Aaron here?" Kyle's mom was speechless. She later called the principal to share the significance of that moment in Kyle's life.

During the week, Kolina gets up at 6:00 every morning. She leaves Kyle's room and makes the rounds of the other bedrooms. If Kyle's mom does not acknowledge her, Kolina gets very vocal—she sings. Kolina then climbs the stairs and repeats this with the boys to make sure everyone is up by 6:15. She is the sweetest alarm clock.

According to Kyle's mom, "God has given me Kyle as a special gift." It has helped her focus on what is important in life—her children. She had to learn about Kyle's world and to adjust her expectations of him. He has only said "I love you" once. Although it was said with no expression, Kyle's mom was thrilled. Kyle says "I love you" in different ways, such as when he lets his mom sit with him, when he holds her face and smiles, and when he brings her a picture.

Kyle may find it difficult making human connections, but he connects with Kolina. Here is unconditional love at its best.

Photo courtesy of Schaffel/Belson Family.

Dundee/Aaron

Dundee

Hannah does not walk independently and has delayed speech. With Dundee's help she is learning about the needs of others.

Hannah's family was terrified about getting a dog. Could they manage this additional responsibility? Hannah's parents and brother Aaron visited Guiding Eyes for the Blind. The family fell in love with Dundee. He had been released from the program due to his sensitivity to certain ground surfaces. His experience of being raised in a classroom helped to create a bond with children.

Hannah's lack of motor control makes it difficult for her to pet Dundee. Thus, her connection to him has been through speech. The family has seen a "speech explosion" since Dundee has become part of the family. He has provided an incredible focus for her. She will inform the family that "Dundee wants a treat. He needs water or needs to go for a walk." Hannah's first word in the morning and her last at night is "Dundee."

Dundee wakes the children up at 6:45 every morning. He clowns around until they go to school. He carries toys and athletic equipment around, ensuring his share of the attention.

Dundee has had an added benefit. He has made Aaron immensely popular with the boys and girls at school and in the neighborhood. Aaron describes his relationship with Dundee as more of a brother than a pet. However, Dundee thinks of Aaron as his playmate. According to Aaron, "Dundee creates a more positive and playful environment at home."

Dundee has not only touched the lives of Hannah and Aaron, but the tight-knit neighborhood they live in. Many of the local children visit with Dundee before they go off to school. Dundee's love is like a magnet, giving these children who may be experiencing their own pain, a safe harbor.

Photo courtesy of Guiding Eyes for the Blind.

Geoff/Ken Venturi

Geoff

Geoff, a yellow Lab, kept pulling at the leg of Ken's pants, while he sat and read. "What's the matter boy?" Ken asked. The second time, Ken admonished Geoff s unusual behavior with, "Stop that." Geoff kept looking at Ken, then started backing toward the other end of the house where Ken's wife, Beau, slept. Ken stood and followed Geoff down the hall toward the master bedroom.

Geoff approached the bed and placed his front paws near Beau's pillow. As he looked from Beau to Ken, Beau opened her eyes briefly. With great love, Ken gathered her in his arms while she took her final breath.

Geoff somehow sensed Beau's final days. As time began to run out, he started a vigil where he would frequently check on her. He walked back and forth down the hall very slowly, as if he was deep in thought. When the ambulance took Beau, Geoff never left the front door. He just waited.

Guiding Eyes for the Blind arranges programs at various golf tournaments to solicit donations and puppy raisers. Celebrities volunteer their time to participate in these programs.

Ken Venturi, the well-known professional golfer, has been raising money for Guiding Eyes for the past twenty-four years. At a golf tournament held at the Whipporwill Country Club, in Westchester County, New York, about eleven years ago, Ken was being interviewed for a Guiding Eyes film clip and was handed a pup, an eight-week-old, furry ball of love. The photo shoot was to be followed by an interview. Once the shoot was finished, he placed the puppy on the grass. It wasn't long before he felt something at his foot.

He looked down to see the puppy patting his foot with his paw. Ken then walked up to the clubhouse where a TV crew waited for him. As he was talking, he felt that familiar paw on his foot. There was the puppy sitting on his foot, looking up at him. He turned to his wife Beau, and told her he had made a friend.

Guiding Eyes for the Blind offered the puppy to Ken in appreciation for his generous work. Ken happily accepted and named the pup Geoff, after a dear friend. Geoff was always Ken's dog. When Ken was not traveling and was home, there was Geoff not just at his feet, but on his feet. They went everywhere together. He accompanied Ken to the club to hit golf balls. He would sit about ten feet away from Ken and relished a ride in the golf cart. He had his own seat in the van. However, as soon as Ken exited the van, Geoff would jump over the back seat and sit in the driver's seat, so that he could keep an eye on Ken. As soon as Ken returned, Geoff took his place in his own seat in the back.

Ken was a natural athlete. When he was eighteen, he was scouted by the New York Yankees and was offered a contract to play with them. He had to make a choice. He chose golf.

He was thirteen years old when he had the opportunity to see Byron Nelson play golf (after Byron had won the San Francisco Open) and told his mother that he wanted to be just like him. Eight years later, Byron Nelson took Ken under his wing and taught him all about the sport.

Ken was a loner, and golf gave him the comfort of solitude. When he was a child, he developed a speech impediment, and was told his stammer was incurable. He could barely say his own name. As a left-handed child, he had been forced to become right-handed which, he feels, created the imbalance affecting his speech. While he practiced golf alone, he worked on his speech. Hard work and perseverance enabled him to overcome this handicap while he developed his golf game.

Ken Venturi's playing career took off in 1956, when he led the Master's after three rounds, attempting to become the first amateur ever to win this prestigious tournament.

He won the 1964 US Open, battling heat exhaustion on the thirty-sixth hole on the final day at the Congressional Country Club. In addition to the 1964 Open, he was selected to join the Ryder Cup Team and received the PGA Player of the Year Award. He developed carpal tunnel syndrome, which became so severe that he was forced to retire from the PGA tour at the age of thirty-seven. He has been a golf analyst for *CBS Sports* for the last thirty-five years.

Besides his work with Guiding Eyes for the Blind, Ken has helped to raise money for abandoned children in Los Angeles, California; Hospice on Marco Island, Florida; Down's syndrome children in Ireland; and Proton (prostate cancer research) in California. He is humble about his generous charity work. According to Ken, "When you give to charity, there are only two people who need to know—you and the man upstairs." He feels his contribution is small compared to the contribution made by the staff at Guiding Eyes for the Blind who dedicate their lives to training these magnificent dogs.

Geoff died of epilepsy at the age of eleven, just three months after Beau. He is buried at her feet, forever watching over her.

Photo courtesy of Rappaport Family.

Sailor

Sailor

Sailor, the handsome black Labrador retriever, was a legend in his time. He fathered 338 puppies. Many were Guiding Eyes for the Blind's best.

If you had ever visited the Canine Development Center over the years, chances are you had met Sailor. When he had been there to "work," this mellow fellow had been granted special privileges of being allowed to circulate in the office and the kitchen. He was a king. Sailor always made himself at home and could often be seen in a completely relaxed position, lying stretched out on his back. However, his signature pose is one where he crossed his front paws, the left paw over the right. This unusual pose has found its way into the genes of many of his puppies. Sailor carried the dominant black gene, which means that all of his puppies are black.

Sailor happened to be in residence at the Canine Development Center when he turned ten. The staff had a birthday party in his honor, complete with balloons, a card, and a cake decorated with miniature dog biscuits. Sailor politely participated in the festivities, then sauntered down the hall carrying a biscuit in his mouth. While the staff continued to celebrate, he found a quiet spot, curled up and went to sleep. Guess there was too much excitement for one day.

Sailor lived to the ripe old age of thirteen and a half. He produced a total of forty-four litters; out of which 179 became guide dogs and thirty-five became breeding stock, all for Guiding Eyes for the Blind.

Printed in the United States
75860LV00002B/1-150